# HOW TO MAKE A
# HUMAN

It all starts
with one cell . . .

WRITTEN BY CLIVE GIFFORD

ILLUSTRATED BY VANJA KRAGULJ

EARTHAWARE
KIDS

Written by Clive Gifford
Illustrated by Vanja Kragulj

Developed and edited by Sue Grabham
Developed and designed by Lee-May Lim

Published by EarthAware Kids
Created by Weldon Owen Children's Books
A subsidiary of Insight International, L.P.

PO Box 3088
San Rafael, CA 94912
www.insighteditions.com

Insight Editions
Publisher: Raoul Goff
Senior Production Manager: Greg Steffen

ISBN: 979-8-88674-100-1

Printed in China
First printing July 2024 DRM0724

10 9 8 7 6 5 4 3 2 1

FSC
www.fsc.org
MIX
Paper | Supporting
responsible forestry
FSC® C188448

# CONTENTS

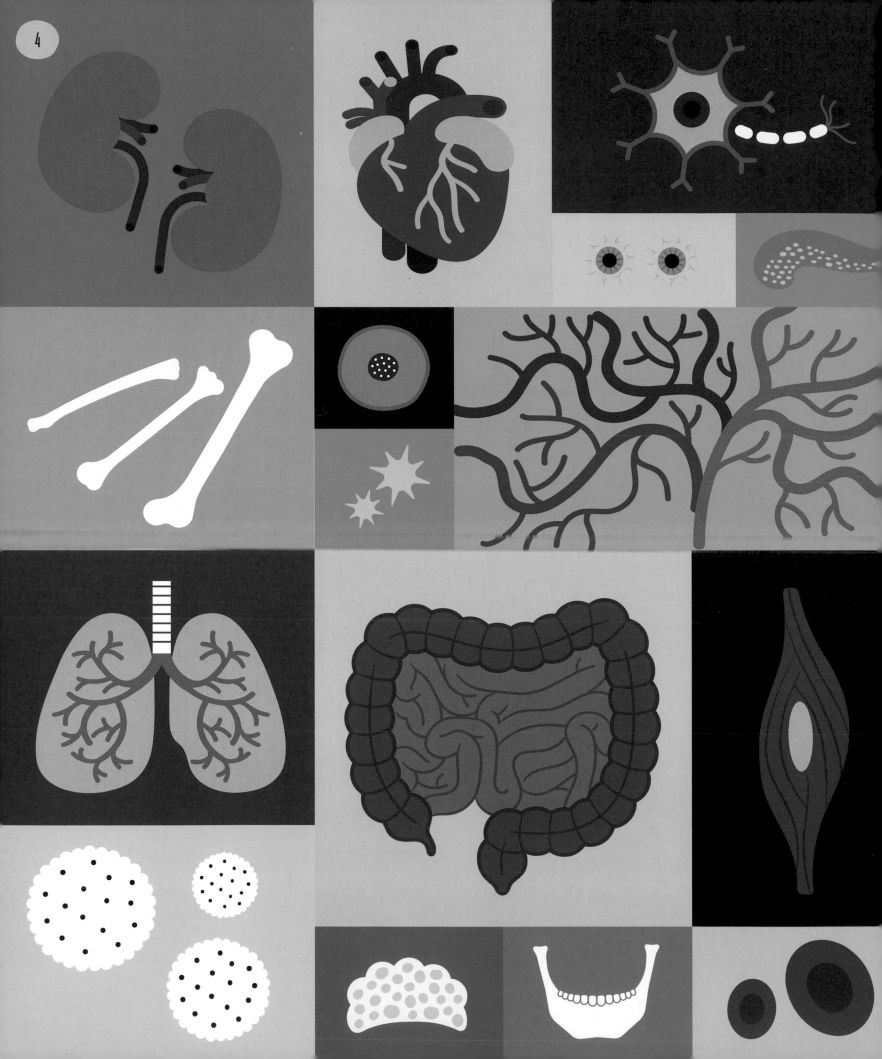

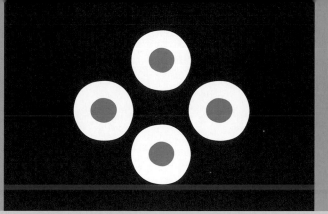

# HOW TO MAKE A HUMAN

Relax. You can't actually make a whole human body from scratch. But it's fun to imagine how it would go if you could. Would you be able to fit all the different gooey, squidgy, bony, muscly, and smelly bits together and make them work? Could you tell your spleen from your sternum and your kidneys from your canines? How would you wire up the brain to the rest of the body? And where would you store all the waste the body creates?

This is the place to imagine building a human from scratch. You'll get to explore all the body's key parts—inside and out—and discover what each bit does. You'll also find out how the bits and pieces connect to form incredible systems that give the body amazing abilities. And that's not all. You'll learn how to look after a human body to keep it working well. Happy body building!

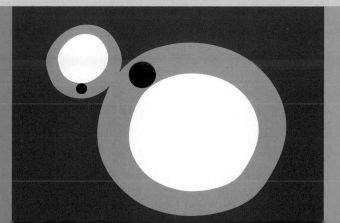
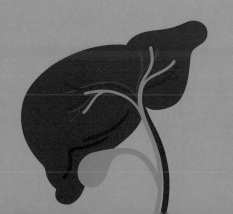

# INGREDIENTS

The human body is a marvelous machine. An incredibly large number of different ingredients and parts are needed to make one. There are all the bits you can see on the outside, from two eyes and two ears to one nose and ten toes. Then, there are the 100,000 hairs on the head and another five million hairs all over the body. And that's just the start—there's far more going on underneath the stretchy skin that holds everything in!

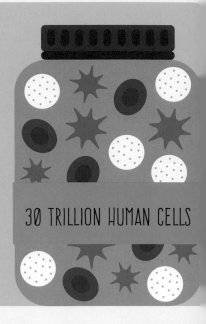

30 TRILLION HUMAN CELLS

206 BONES

1 HEART

1 LIVER, 1 GALL BLADDER

1 SPLEEN

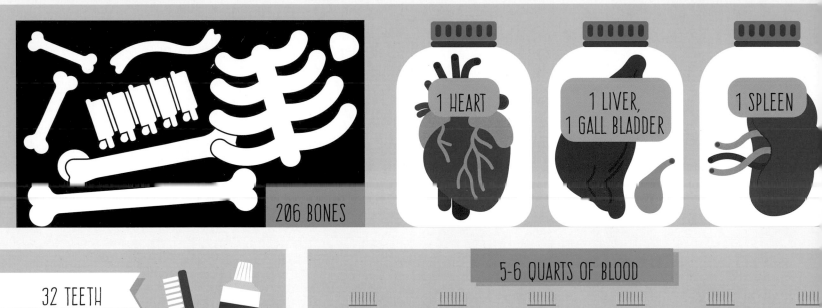

32 TEETH

5-6 QUARTS OF BLOOD

650 MUSCLES

100,000 MILES OF BLOOD VESSELS

THYMUS, THYROID, ADRENAL GLAND

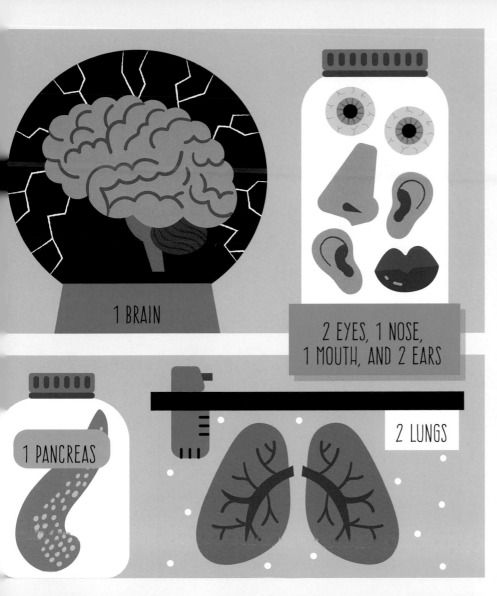

1 BRAIN

2 EYES, 1 NOSE,
1 MOUTH, AND 2 EARS

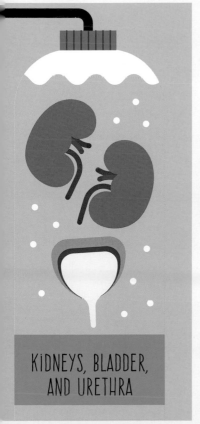

1 PANCREAS

2 LUNGS

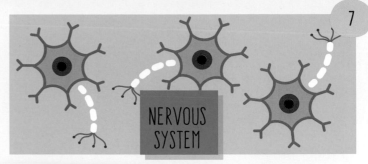

NERVOUS SYSTEM

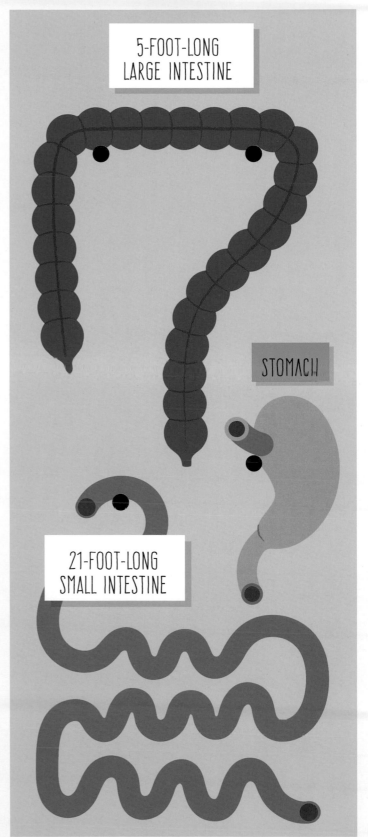

5-FOOT-LONG
LARGE INTESTINE

STOMACH

21-FOOT-LONG
SMALL INTESTINE

NAILS

SKIN

HAIR

KIDNEYS, BLADDER,
AND URETHRA

# BUILDING BLOCKS

Cells are the building blocks from which every living animal and plant is made. Most human body cells are so small that you could fit 20 or 30 of them across a period on this page . . . with room to spare! So, it's mind-blowing to think that every human started out as one single, teensy-tiny cell. This divided in two. Then, those two cells divided into four and so on, and so on.

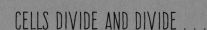

CELLS DIVIDE AND DIVIDE . . .

+ = 2

. . . AND MULTIPLY

AND MULTIPLY . . .

+ = 4

+ = 8

. . . UNTIL A FULLY GROWN PERSON HAS ABOUT 30 TRILLION HUMAN CELLS!

## TYPES OF CELLS

How many different types of cells do you think a human body needs? Ten? Twenty? To build a human, there need to be more than 200 different types of cells. Here are some of the most important ones:

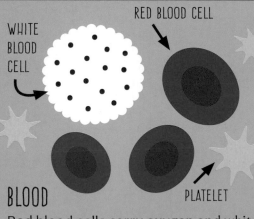

WHITE BLOOD CELL
RED BLOOD CELL
PLATELET

### BLOOD
Red blood cells carry oxygen and white blood cells fight infection. Platelets are fragments of cells also found in blood.

### BONE
These spiky cells make human bones hard and strong. They also help to form new bone.

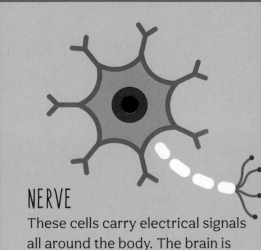

### NERVE
These cells carry electrical signals all around the body. The brain is packed with over 85 billion of them!

## WHAT IS A CELL?

Cells are the smallest working parts of living things. Each of these tiny parcels of chemicals has a nucleus. This bosses other parts of the cell around to do their job.

Surrounding the nucleus is a jelly called cytoplasm. Keeping the cell together is a thin wall called a membrane, which lets some things in and other substances out.

Once upon a time I was just ONE cell!

CELL

CYTOPLASM

NUCLEUS

MEMBRANE

WOW!

## MUSCLE

Thin, long, and strong, these cells club together to form the muscles that make the human body move.

## FAT

These cells can e-x-p-a-n-d like balloons. They store fat, which is a great source of energy for the body.

## SKIN

These cells only live for two to four weeks but do a vital job. They protect the body from the world outside.

# LET'S GET ORGANIZED

It may look like chaos inside, but the human body is an absolute marvel of organization. It is packed with thousands and thousands of parts, some hard and tough, others soft and squelchy. These are all arranged into different systems, which have their own important jobs to do. The systems rely on each other to keep the body working well and in great shape. If it really was possible to make your own human body, it would be sensible to work on the systems one at a time.

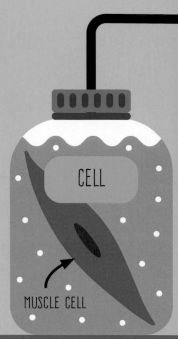

CELL

MUSCLE CELL

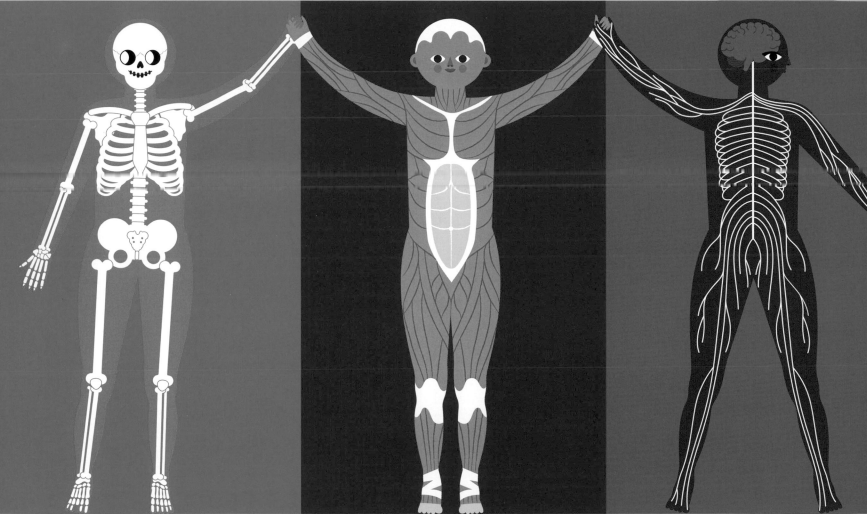

## SKELETAL SYSTEM
The body's weight is supported by a bony frame. This system gives the body its shape, allows movement, and protects delicate organs such as the heart.

## MUSCULAR SYSTEM
Power, strength, and movement are produced by this amazing system. More than 600 muscles allow movement by pulling the body parts around.

## NERVOUS SYSTEM
This information network sends millions of tiny electrical signals to and from the brain so that it can sense and control all the body's parts.

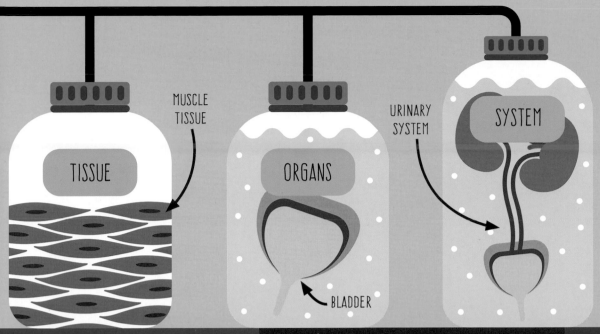

## FROM CELLS TO SYSTEMS

Similar cells group together to form tissue such as muscle.

Different tissues combine to form important organs such as the bladder.

An organ works with other tissues and organs in a system. The bladder, for example, is part of the urinary system, which removes liquid waste from the body.

MUSCLE TISSUE

TISSUE

ORGANS

URINARY SYSTEM

SYSTEM

BLADDER

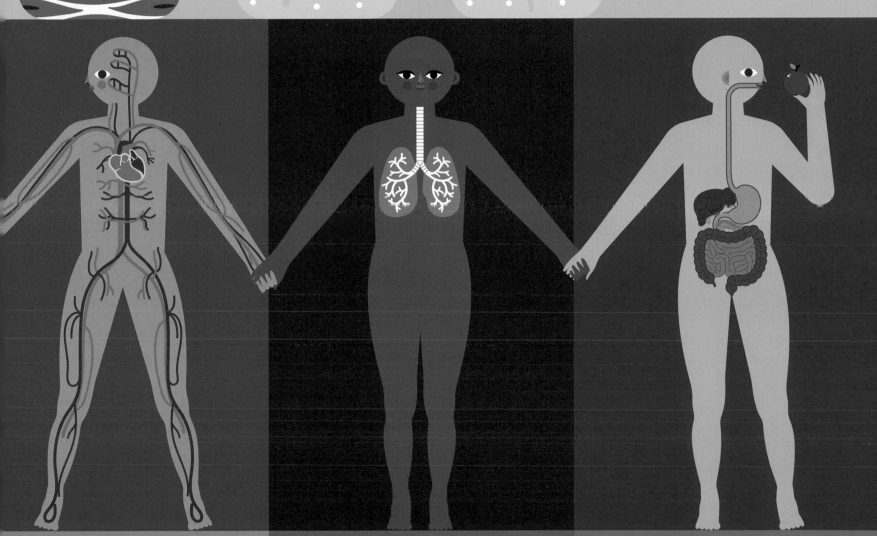

## CIRCULATORY SYSTEM

Blood circulates, or travels, around the body in a network of tubes called blood vessels. Blood is pumped by the tireless heart muscle in the chest.

## RESPIRATORY SYSTEM

Some 2,100–2,400 gallons of air enter the body every day through the respiratory, or breathing, system. It carries oxygen into the body and waste gases out.

## DIGESTIVE SYSTEM

This system digests, or breaks down, food so the body can make energy. The body absorbs nutrients from food to keep itself strong and healthy.

# AMAZING FRAME

To make sure a human body isn't floppy, it needs a frame inside–the skeleton. This supports, protects, and moves the body. It is made up of lots of bones of different shapes and sizes. Bone is a remarkable material. It is lighter than many metals, yet stronger. What's more, unlike other materials, bone is alive– it can mend itself if it is damaged.

A baby is born with around 300 bones, but many of these fuse, or join together, as the human grows up. A typical adult human has 206 bones altogether.

SPINE

### BENDY BACKBONE
Adult humans have 24 irregular-shaped bones in their spine, or backbone, called vertebrae. This tall stack of bones is strong but flexible.

## HOW MANY BONES?

$$48 + 32 + 90 + 36 = 206$$

| flat bones | short bones | long bones | irregular bones | bones altogether |

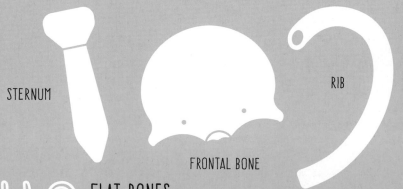

STERNUM

RIB

FRONTAL BONE

### 48 FLAT BONES
These form the skull and rib cage, acting as body armor to protect more delicate parts. They also provide lots of places to attach muscles.

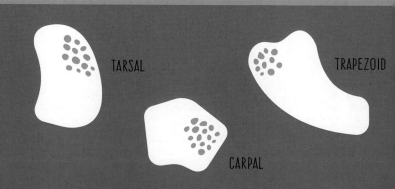

TARSAL

TRAPEZOID

CARPAL

### 32 SHORT BONES
Many short bones are found in the wrists and ankles, where they slide over one another to allow feet and hands to move.

## AMAZING!

### WHAT'S INSIDE A BONE?

Below the surface of a bone lies hard, strong layers of compact bone, then lightweight spongy bone full of little hollows. In the middle there are blood vessels and bone marrow, which makes two million red blood cells every second.

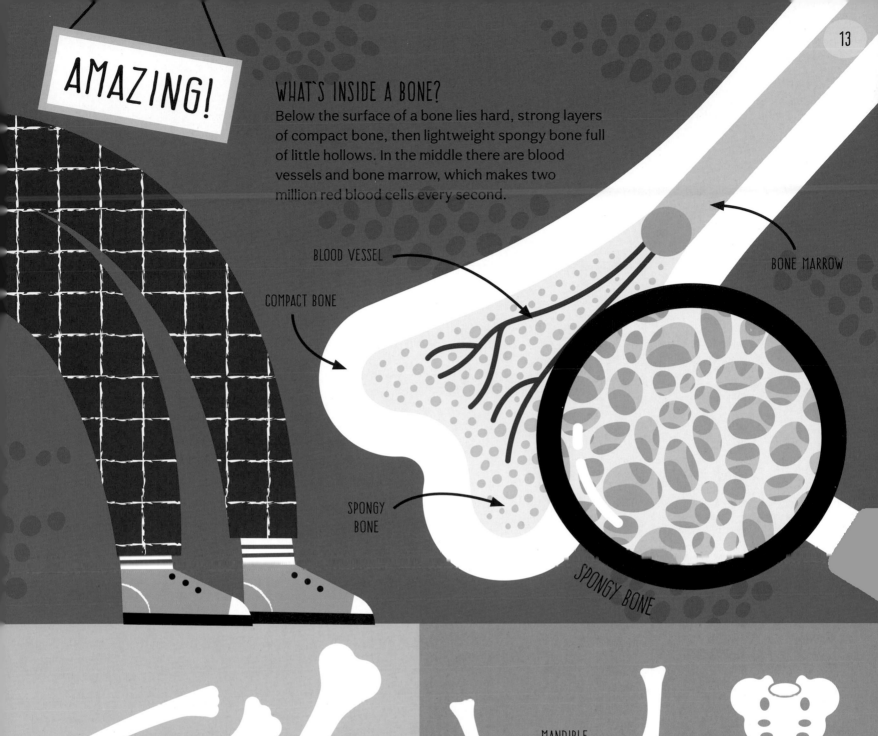

BLOOD VESSEL

COMPACT BONE

SPONGY BONE

BONE MARROW

SPONGY BONE

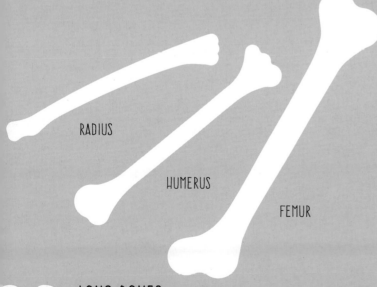

RADIUS

HUMERUS

FEMUR

### 90 LONG BONES

These are mostly found in arms, legs, and fingers. The longest long bone is the femur, or thighbone, which is roughly a quarter of a person's height.

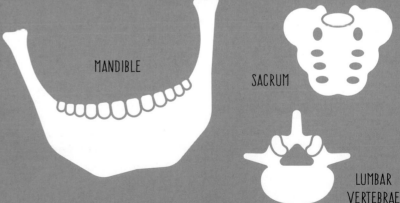

MANDIBLE

SACRUM

LUMBAR VERTEBRAE

### 36 IRREGULAR BONES

This mixed bag of bones includes the vertebrae, which make up the spine, the bones of the face, and the mandible, or lower jawbone.

SOME PEOPLE HAVE EXTRA RIBS, VERTEBRAE, TOES, OR FINGERS!

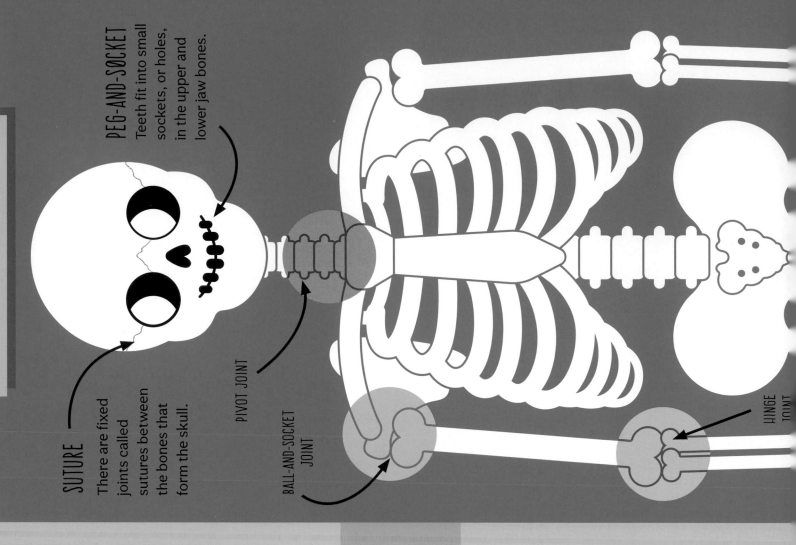

**PEG-AND-SOCKET**
Teeth fit into small sockets, or holes, in the upper and lower jaw bones.

**SUTURE**
There are fixed joints called sutures between the bones that form the skull.

PIVOT JOINT

BALL-AND-SOCKET JOINT

HINGE JOINT

# A GIANT JIGSAW

The human skeleton is like a giant and complicated 3D jigsaw puzzle. More than half the 206 bones in the body are found in the hands and feet. There are also 24 bones in the spine and another 24 in the rib cage–plus bones in the arms, legs, knees, shoulders, head, and pelvis. Each bone is important and needs to fit in just the right place.

Bones meet at places called joints. Some, like the joints in the skull, are fixed. Others let the bones move freely.

## MOVING JOINTS

Different moving joints allow different amounts of movement. They hold bones together but allow them to move when muscles pull them.

**BALL-AND-SOCKET**

**HINGE**

Used in the shoulders and hips, ball-and-socket joints let arms and legs move freely in almost any direction.

Found in the knees, elbows, and fingers, hinge joints allow movement in only one direction, just like the hinges on a door.

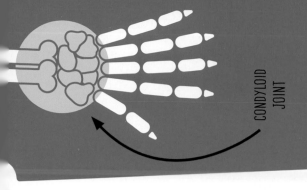

CONDYLOID JOINT

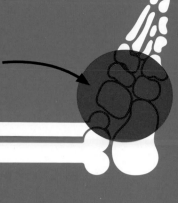

PLANE JOINT

SADDLE JOINT

## FOOT

There are 26 bones in each foot. These form 33 joints held in place by lots of tiny ligaments.

## PLANE

The flat bone surfaces in plane joints glide over each other, allowing just a little movement.

## PIVOT

In pivot joints, one bone rotates around the other, allowing the neck, wrists, and elbows to turn from side to side.

## CONDYLOID

Found in wrists and heels, these are a little like ball-and-socket joints but with less range of movement.

## SADDLE

The saddle joint allows bones to move back and forth and from side to side but with no turring or twisting.

## STAYING IN PLACE

Ligaments are tough cords that hold bones in place in a joint.

The ends of many bones are covered in smooth, shiny cartilage, which protects the bones as they rub against each other.

## WEAR AND TEAR

Cartilage is strong and flexible. It protects the bones that move inside joints such as knees.

CARTILAGE

LIGAMENT

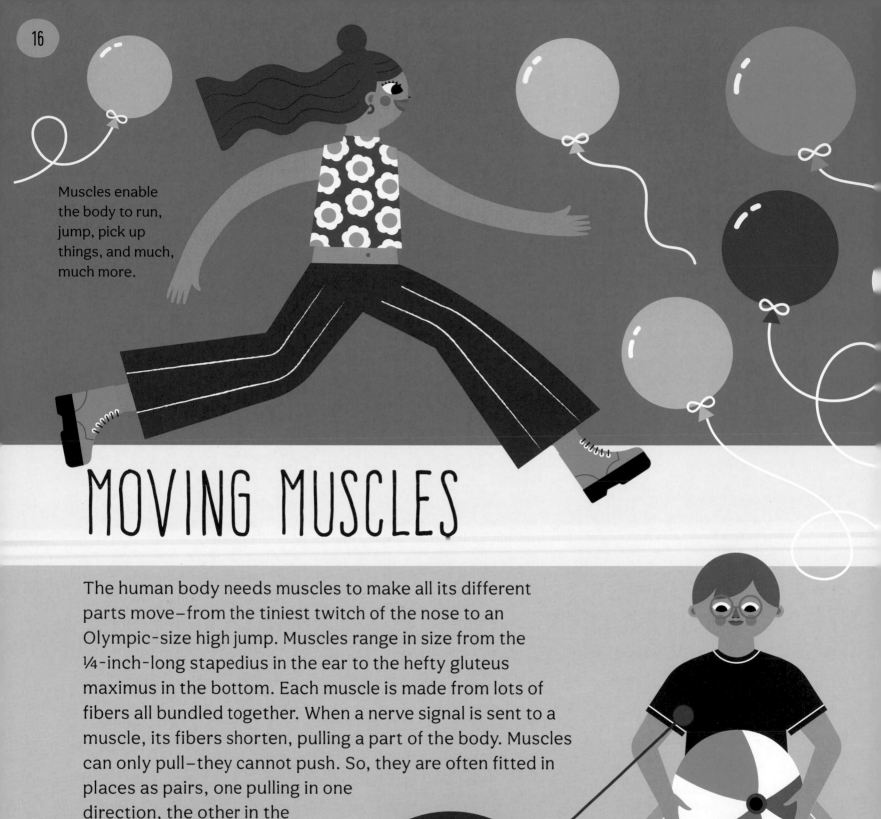

Muscles enable the body to run, jump, pick up things, and much, much more.

# MOVING MUSCLES

The human body needs muscles to make all its different parts move—from the tiniest twitch of the nose to an Olympic-size high jump. Muscles range in size from the ¼-inch-long stapedius in the ear to the hefty gluteus maximus in the bottom. Each muscle is made from lots of fibers all bundled together. When a nerve signal is sent to a muscle, its fibers shorten, pulling a part of the body. Muscles can only pull—they cannot push. So, they are often fitted in places as pairs, one pulling in one direction, the other in the opposite direction.

## LIFTING ARM
The biceps shortens to bend and raise the lower arm. The triceps muscle stays loose and relaxed.

BICEPS

TRICEPS

# MUSCLE MAP

Most of the body is covered in muscles. There are more than 600 of them altogether! Skeletal muscles are attached to the bones in the skeleton to make them move. They are attached with strong, springy cords called tendons.

SKELETAL MUSCLE

DELTOID MUSCLE

TENDONS

# STRAIGHT ARM

To straighten the arm, the biceps relaxes. The triceps shortens and pulls the arm down.

BICEPS

TRICEPS

# MUSCLE NAMES

The ancient Greeks and Romans were the first to study muscles, which is why many are named in Latin. *Deltoid* means "triangular-shaped."

TIBALIS MUSCLE

# TYPES OF MUSCLE

There are three different muscle types. Skeletal muscles move the bones, while hardworking cardiac muscle is found inside the heart, keeping it beating all the time. Smooth muscle makes organs such as the intestines work, squeezing food and waste through the body.

CARDIAC MUSCLE

SMOOTH MUSCLE

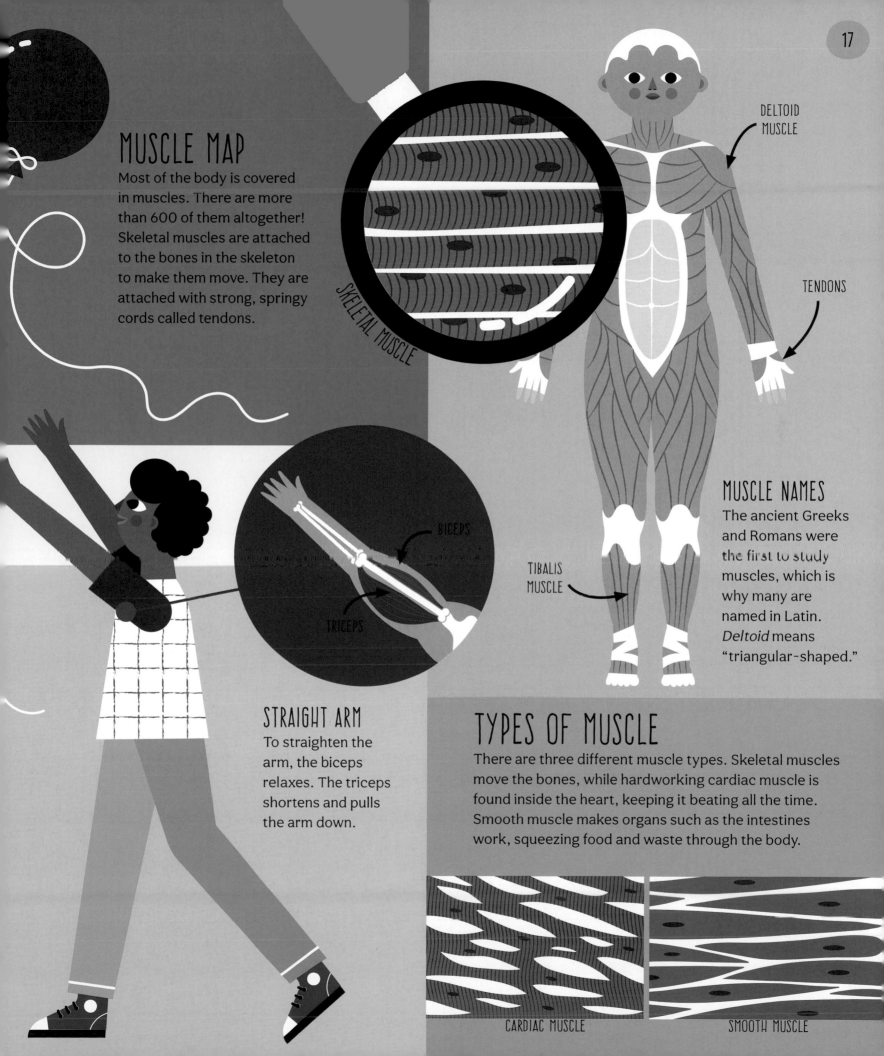

# MUSCLE HEAD

There are more than 50 muscles, large and small, in the neck, head, and face. The tongue alone contains eight! Some of these muscles help to bite and chew food. Others move the eyes or make them blink or squint. Two small muscles on either side of the mouth, called buccinators, help people to puff out their cheeks.

Many of the muscles in the head pull the skin on the face from the inside to produce a wide range of funny faces. Scientists call these facial expressions. They are used to communicate with others without speaking. So, others know when someone is happy, sad, angry, surprised, or sulking just by looking at them.

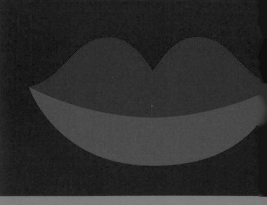

### SMILE
The zygomaticus major, or happy muscle, helps pull the corners of the mouth up into a smile.

### OPEN WIDE!
The masseter is the strongest muscle the body. It works with other muscles open and close the jaw and mouth.

### BLOW A KISS
A circular muscle called the orbicularis oris helps to close the mouth and pucker up the lips ready for a kiss.

### CHILL OUT
Even at rest, muscles in the head and back are working—for example, to keep the eyes closed or the head level.

### WINK
The body's fastest muscle—the orbiculari oculi—closes the eyelid to wink or blink in less than one-tenth of a second.

## TONGUE OUT!

...superthick muscle – genioglossus – ...needed to poke the tongue out ...make a face or taste something.

## REALLY?

...hen a face shows doubt, many ...uscles are at work. One of them is ...e mentalis, which pulls the chin up.

## FROWN

...rinkles between the eyebrows are ...ade when the corrugator supercilii ...uscles pull the skin upward.

## HAPPY FACE

From widening the eyes and wrinkling the forehead to pulling a broad smile, looking cheerful takes many muscles.

## CRY

It takes 12 muscles to screw up the face and for the lacrimal glands to release tears for a good old sob.

## ACHOO!

Muscles in the body, chest, neck, and eyelids all perform a sneeze, during which the eyes are always closed.

## ANGRY

When someone is angry, facial muscles contract to make the brow frown and the mouth turn down. Other muscles open the eyes wide.

## SURPRISE, SURPRISE!

Pulling at the forehead, the frontalis muscle raises the eyebrows to show surprise or shock at the unexpected.

# THE BRAIN

The human body needs to be told what to do, and that is the job of the busy and buzzing human brain. This super control center comes in two halves—right and left. Each side of the brain needs to know what the other is doing, so it is joined up with a thick bundle of 200 million nerve fibers called the corpus callosum.

## BRAIN BATH

The brain is about the size of a small to medium cauliflower. It sits in about 5 ounces of fluid. This "brain bath" helps to protect it against bumps and shocks.

# KEY BRAIN PARTS

Each brain half has a wrinkly outer layer called the cerebral cortex. Each side is divided up into four lobes. Below the cortex are two vital parts that do crucial work without the human even thinking about them—the cerebellum and the brain stem.

### FRONTAL LOBES

These lobes allow the brain to plan, make decisions, think up new ideas, and solve problems. Epic!

+

### PARIETAL LOBES

These manage the senses of taste and touch and help the body to carry out complicated movements.

+

### OCCIPITAL LOBES

These make sense of all the information sent by the eyes such as recognizing objects and colors.

+

### TEMPORAL LOBES

The temporal lobes handl hearing, understand language, and help form long-term memories.

CORPUS CALLOSUM

## BRAIN POWER

The brain only makes up one-fiftieth of the body's weight yet uses one-fifth of all the body's energy. That's because it's got so much to do. The brain handles all the body's senses, has thoughts and ideas, and stores memories to recognize faces. It also recalls facts and learns super skills such as playing music or riding a bike.

## CROSSOVER

The brain's right half controls the left-hand side of the body, while its left half controls the right side.

## CEREBELLUM

This commands all the muscles so the body stays upright and balanced.

+

## BRAIN STEM

This connects the brain to the body. It also controls breathing, heartbeats, and swallowing.

=

## THE BRAIN

FRONTAL LOBE

PARIETAL LOBE

OCCIPITAL LOBE

TEMPORAL LOBE

BRAIN STEM

CEREBELLUM

# NERVE NETWORK

Nerves are the body's main messaging system, and humans need more than 40 miles of them! Nerves send millions of signals as tiny pulses of electricity every day.

Each nerve is made up of cells called neurons. One neuron passes on a signal to the next neuron using chemicals to cross the gap between them. This system is fast—some signals travel at 250 miles per hour—faster than a racing car!

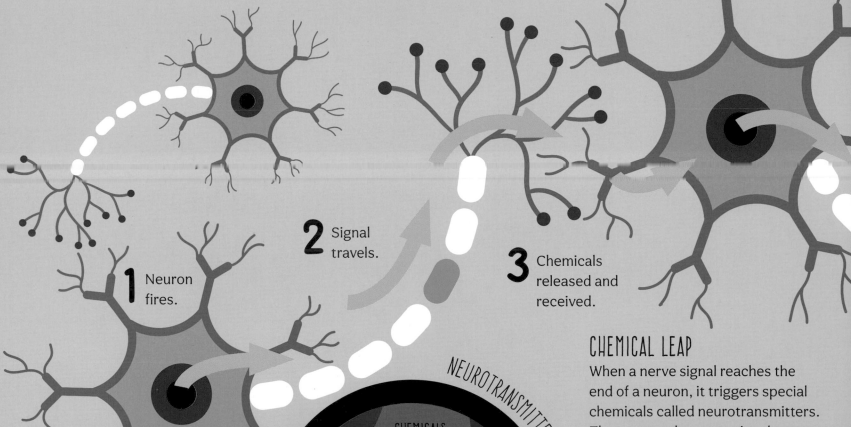

**1** Neuron fires.

**2** Signal travels.

**3** Chemicals released and received.

NEUROTRANSMITTERS

CHEMICALS RELEASED

CHEMICALS RECEIVED

## CHEMICAL LEAP

When a nerve signal reaches the end of a neuron, it triggers special chemicals called neurotransmitters. These carry the nerve signal across the gap to the next neuron.

# IT'S ELECTRIC! ⚡

## CONNECTING UP

Each neuron has tiny, branching fingers called dendrites. These can pick up the chemicals sent by nerve signals from dozens of other neurons.

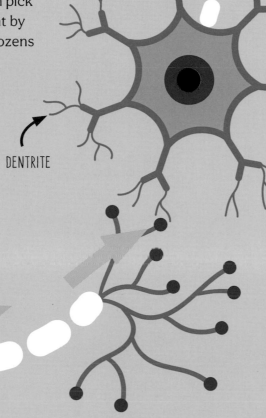

DENTRITE

**4** Signal travels along next neuron.

## TWO-WAY TRAFFIC

Nerves carry information signals from parts of the body back to the brain. They tell the brain how the body part is doing. In return, the brain sends out millions of command signals that travel along nerves throughout the body.

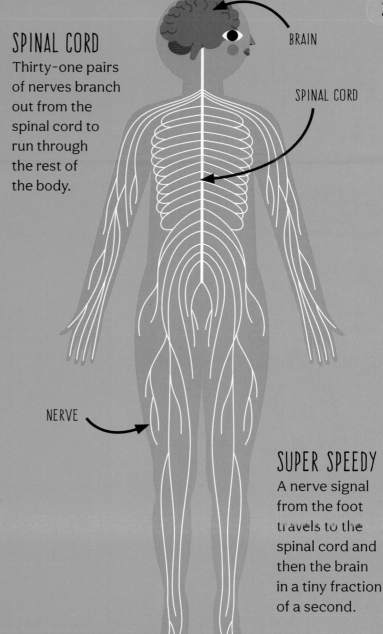

## SPINAL CORD

Thirty-one pairs of nerves branch out from the spinal cord to run through the rest of the body.

BRAIN

SPINAL CORD

NERVE

## SUPER SPEEDY

A nerve signal from the foot travels to the spinal cord and then the brain in a tiny fraction of a second.

## CENTRAL NERVOUS SYSTEM

The brain and the spinal cord form the central nervous system. Dozens of outer nerves spread out through the body, carrying signals to and from the spinal cord.

## REFLEX ACTION

The spinal cord commands a body part to withdraw from something sharp or hot. This reflex action is automatic and does not involve the brain.

# CHEMICAL MESSAGES

With so many signals and messages needed to make the body work well, it's no wonder the nervous system needs help! The human body has a second messaging service—the endocrine system. This uses chemicals called hormones instead of electricity.

Hormones are released by different organs all over the body. But it all starts in the brain. When signals reach the pea-sized but very bossy pituitary gland, it sends out orders to the organs called glands. The glands then release their specialized hormones to tell particular cells what to do.

## SUGAR CONTROL

Glucose from food is the body's main fuel. Hormones from the pancreas manage how much glucose is in the blood.

## T-CELL TRAINER

The thymus trains white blood cells to become T-cells, which travel round the blood fighting diseases and infections.

## GROW, GROW, GROW

The pituitary gland produces growth hormone. This encourages bone and cartilage to keep on growing.

## HIGHS AND LOWS

The hypothalamus controls activity in the pituitary. It helps keep the body balanced, avoiding ups and downs.

## READY FOR ACTION!

When someone is stressed or scared, the adrenal glands' hormones produce energy to make the heart beat faster.

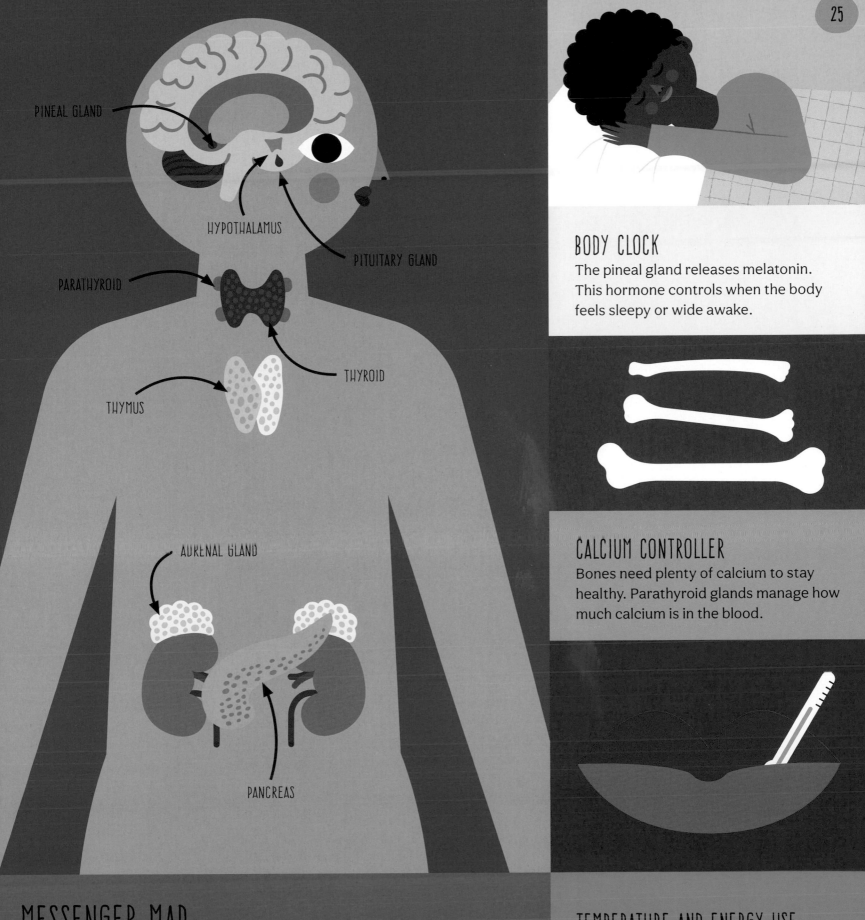

## PINEAL GLAND

## HYPOTHALAMUS

## PITUITARY GLAND

## PARATHYROID

## THYROID

## THYMUS

## ADRENAL GLAND

## PANCREAS

## BODY CLOCK
The pineal gland releases melatonin. This hormone controls when the body feels sleepy or wide awake.

## CALCIUM CONTROLLER
Bones need plenty of calcium to stay healthy. Parathyroid glands manage how much calcium is in the blood.

## MESSENGER MAP
More than 40 different hormones are made by glands. Most hormones travel through blood vessels to reach the cells they want to command. The hypothalamus is a link between the brain and the endocrine system.

## TEMPERATURE AND ENERGY USE
The thyroid's hormones control how fast cells work and how much energy they use. They also control body temperature.

# SIGHT AND EYES

Sight is one of the body's most incredible senses. The eyes are a window to the world, allowing humans to see everything from the tiniest insect to the biggest mountain.

Two eyeballs fit snugly into the orbits, or eye sockets, in the skull. Each eye has a hole in the middle called the pupil, which is surrounded by a colored ring of muscle known as the iris. The iris pattern in every human body is unique, just like a person's fingerprints.

## EYE-MAZING!

**1** Light from an object travels toward the eye.

## INSIDE THE EYE

Light travels through the eye's pupil to reach the retina at the back. There, light-sensitive cells, called rods and cones, convert it into electrical signals. These signals travel along the optic nerve to the brain, which works out what is actually being seen.

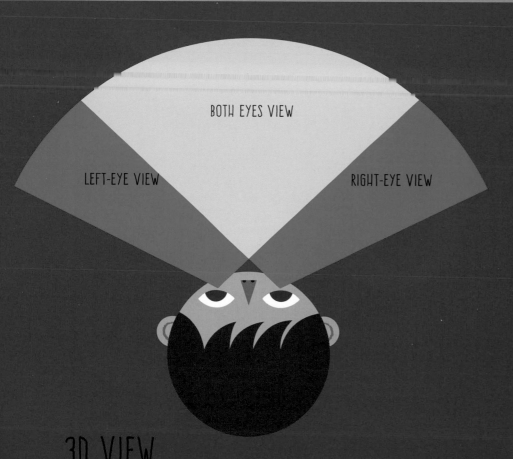

BOTH EYES VIEW

LEFT-EYE VIEW

RIGHT-EYE VIEW

## 3D VIEW

Because both eyes face forward, they both see most of the same scene but from slightly different views. The brain uses these differences to build up a three-dimensional (3D) picture with height, width, and depth.

DISTANT VISION

## FOCUSING

Tiny muscles can change the lens' shape so the eye can focus on objects close by or see more distant objects just as clearly.

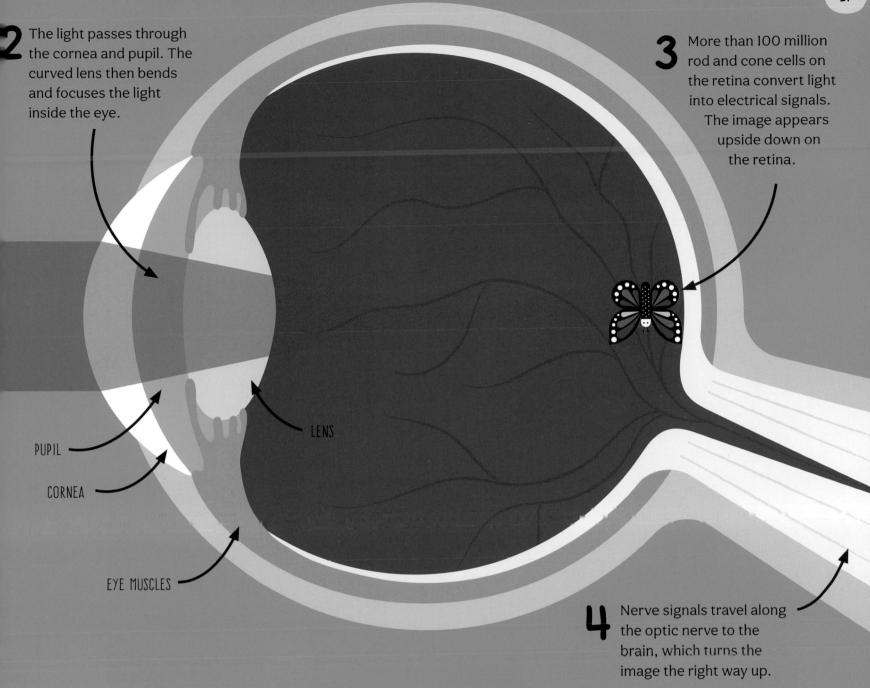

**2** The light passes through the cornea and pupil. The curved lens then bends and focuses the light inside the eye.

**3** More than 100 million rod and cone cells on the retina convert light into electrical signals. The image appears upside down on the retina.

PUPIL

CORNEA

LENS

EYE MUSCLES

**4** Nerve signals travel along the optic nerve to the brain, which turns the image the right way up.

NEAR VISION

DIM LIGHT

PUPIL

IRIS

BRIGHT LIGHT

# BRIGHT AND DIM

In bright light, muscles in the iris shrink the pupil to stop too much light entering the eye. In the dark, the muscles open the pupil wide to let in as much light as possible.

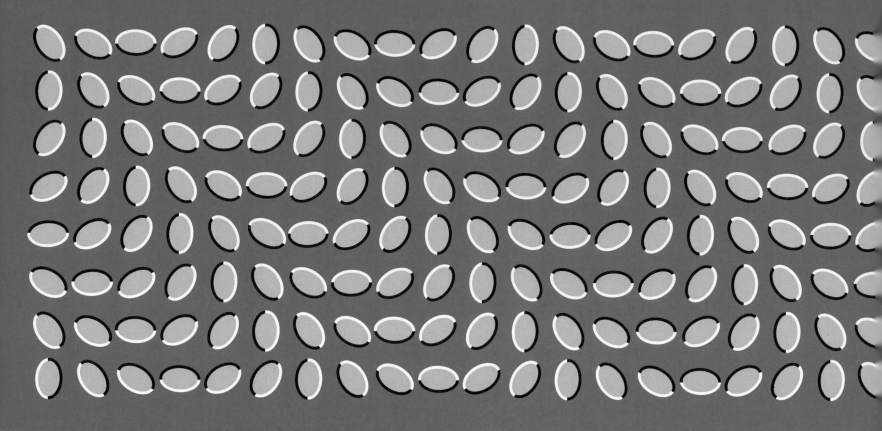

# EYE TEST

The body uses both its eyes and brain to see. Working together, they can give it an amazingly powerful sense of sight. But it is not always perfect. Some eyes need help from glasses or contact lenses, and most humans can be fooled with optical illusions.

Some illusions work because of the way the eyes view objects and their physical limits. Other tricks and illusions occur because of how the brain works. It is bombarded with information from the eyes constantly. So, the brain sometimes makes shortcuts and assumes things to save time, and that is when mistakes creep in.

## TWITCHING EYES

Stare at the picture above. After a few moments, the leaves seem to sway like they're in a video, not a book. Extraordinary! The eyes make tiny twitching movements as they constantly scan and rescan the view in front of them. These, and the shading on the leaves, trick the brain into thinking the leaves are moving.

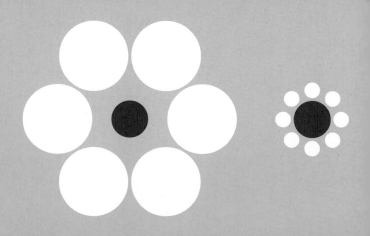

## BRAIN TRICK

Which of the two blue circles is bigger? The right one? Nope. They are both the same size! The brain is tricked, influenced by the surrounding white circles into thinking that the blue disks are different sizes.

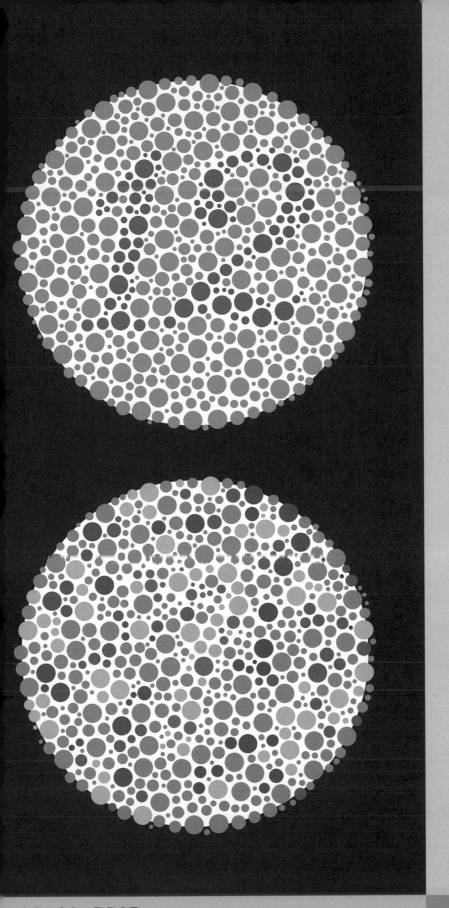

V

T E

L C A

T N X O

O V E H U

U X T L F H

L A O E V K

O U T X H F

## COLOR TEST

Some people's eyes find it difficult to spot differences between certain colors. They may be colorblind. An Ishihara test is a useful way to check this. Special glasses and contact lenses can help with colorblindness.

## EYE TEST

Tests can help to see if a human needs glasses. If the eyeballs are a little out of shape, things close up may appear fuzzy. This is longsighted. If the eyes struggle to view things farther away they are shortsighted.

# HEARING AND EARS

Sounds are vibrations that travel through the air as waves. Ears can detect all sorts of sounds—quiet and loud, music and speech, whispers and bangs. With an ear on either side of the head, the body can work out which direction a sound comes from by the different time it takes to reach each ear.

Nerves from each ear carry sound signals to the brain. It's the brain that allows a human to hear and recognize lots of different sounds all happening at the same time.

EAR FLAP

DON'T WOBBLE!

## STAYING BALANCED

Parts in the inner ear help give the body another sense—balance. Semicircular canals are three tiny tubes, each filled with liquid. As the head moves, the liquid sloshes around and sends signals along the vestibular nerve to the brain. The brain uses this information to adjust the body to stay balanced.

## OUTER EAR

Here, the ear flap gathers in sound waves and channels them down a narrow tube called the ear canal to strike the eardrum. This stretchy skin vibrates as the sounds strike.

SKULL BONE

EAR CANAL

HAMMER

ANVIL

STIRRUP

EARDRUM

SEMICIRCULAR CANALS

COCHLEAR NERVE

COCHLEA

## INSIDE THE EAR

There are three parts to the ear—the outer, middle, and inner. Sound waves take a journey through all three parts. The waves are amplified, or made stronger, then turned into electrical signals sent to the brain.

## MIDDLE EAR

Vibrations trigger the hammer to tap the anvil, which hits the stirrup, making the vibrations stronger.

## INNER EAR

The cochlea is a liquid-filled tube all coiled up like a snail's shell. Inside, vibrations cause ripples that tiny hairs pick up and turn into electrical signals to message the brain.

# SMELL AND TASTE

From stinky socks to sweet perfume and spicy peppers to freshly baked bread, humans come across many smells and tastes. But to sense them, they need a nose and a tongue.

Smell receptor cells at the back of the nose and taste buds on the tongue and in the mouth make smelling and tasting possible. The two senses work together to let humans enjoy many scents and flavors and to warn of dangers such as smoke or rotten food.

## SMELL DETECTION

Some smell, or odor, molecules enter the nose via the nostrils. Others are released when food is chewed, traveling out of the throat and up into the nose.

## TASTES AND FLAVORS

Taste buds recognize five basic tastes, from sweet to umami–a savory flavor found in meat, mushrooms, and cheese. All the different flavors the body senses are made up of combinations of these five.

SALTY

SOUR

SWEET

BITTER

UMAMI

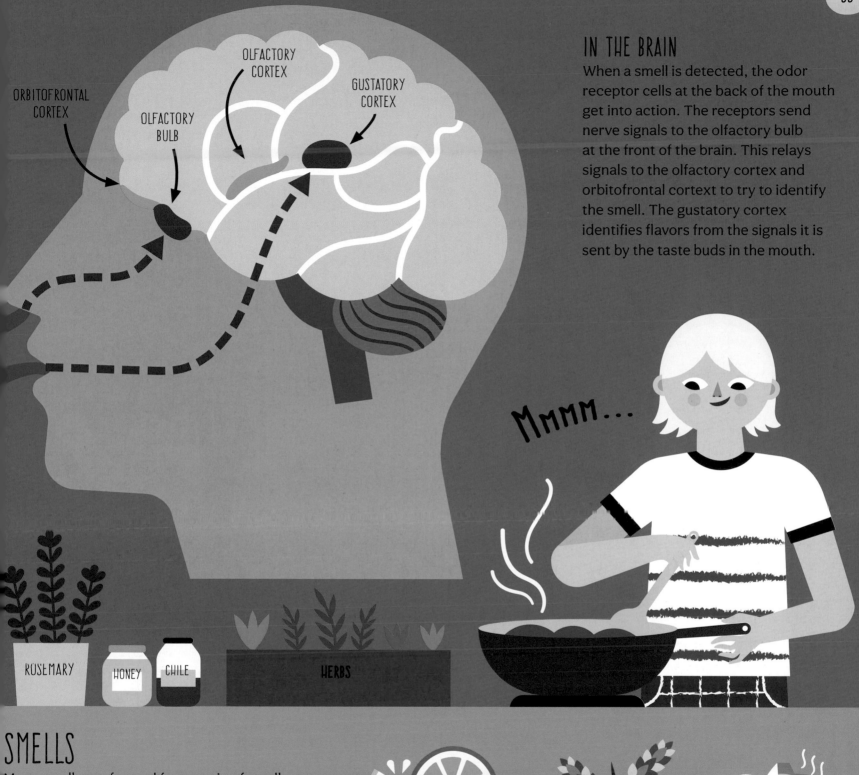

ORBITOFRONTAL
CORTEX

OLFACTORY
BULB

OLFACTORY
CORTEX

GUSTATORY
CORTEX

## IN THE BRAIN

When a smell is detected, the odor receptor cells at the back of the mouth get into action. The receptors send nerve signals to the olfactory bulb at the front of the brain. This relays signals to the olfactory cortex and orbitofrontal cortext to try to identify the smell. The gustatory cortex identifies flavors from the signals it is sent by the taste buds in the mouth.

Mmmm...

ROSEMARY

HONEY CHILE

HERBS

# SMELLS

Many smells are formed from a mix of smell, or odor, molecules. Scientists group smells into categories including woody, pungent, and fruity. Every nose has a slightly different mix of odor receptors, so each person may sense some smells differently.

CITRUS

FLORAL

DECAYED

CHEMICAL

PUNGENT    WOODY

FRUITY

# THE HEART

The body needs a powerful, nonstop pump—a heart. The human heart is about the size of an adult human's fist and made of layers of solid, strong cardiac muscle. It sits deep in the chest and is protected by the bony rib cage and sternum, or breastbone. The heart is a tireless workhorse. Instructed by nerve signals, it will continue to beat, every minute, day and night, for the entire time the human is alive.

Each day, the heart beats around 100,000 times. Each beat pushes a small amount of blood out of its chambers and along tubes called arteries that branch off to serve every part of the body.

**LUB-DUB, LUB-DUB**

### HEART RATE

A healthy heart beats 60 to 100 times a minute when the body is at rest. When the body is running or exercising hard, it can increase to 150 or 160 beats per minute.

# BLOOD

This sticky liquid is essential for every human. It whizzes around a network of tubes called blood vessels. Along the way, blood delivers oxygen and other important chemicals to different parts of the body. It also carries away waste substances.

### RED BLOOD CELLS

These cells contain a substance called hemoglobin, which stores oxygen and gives blood its red color. A one-twenty-fifth-inch-wide drop of blood can contain over 5,000,000 red blood cells.

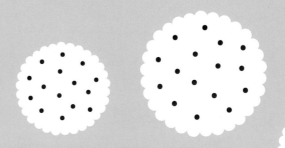

### WHITE BLOOD CELLS

Just 1 percent of blood is made up of these germ- and infection-fighting cells. They are made in bone marrow and found in the blood and in other tissues.

## FROM THE BODY
This large vein is called the superior vena cava. It returns blood low in oxygen to the heart.

TO THE BODY

## TO THE LUNGS
The blood is pumped through the heart and out to the lungs, where it will gain lots of oxygen.

LEFT ATRIUM

FROM THE LUNGS

## FROM THE LUNGS
Blood full of oxygen from the lungs returns to the heart to be pumped around the rest of the body.

RIGHT ATRIUM

LEFT VENTRICLE

## THE PUMP
The heart is really two pumps in one. It contains left and right pairs of chambers. The two right chambers move blood to the lungs. The left pair pump the now oxygen-rich blood returning from the lungs all around the body.

RIGHT VENTRICLE

THE HEART BEATS AROUND 36,500,000 TIMES A YEAR!

FROM THE BODY

## PLATELETS
These colorless fragments of cells are made in marrow inside bones. They help blood to thicken and to form a clot to seal a wound from a cut or a graze.

## PLASMA
This thin, watery liquid makes up just over half of blood. It is light yellow and carries salts and many other vital nutrients around the body.

# TRANSPORT NETWORK

Every human body has a super-long internal transport network made up of thousands of long, narrow tubes called blood vessels. Inside this mazy network of vessels, blood flows to the brain, hands, feet, and every other part of the body. The blood supplies body parts with nutrients and oxygen. It also collects waste, whisking away unwanted substances. Each human body needs over 60,000 miles of blood vessels. Laid out end to end, they would circle the Earth two and a half times!

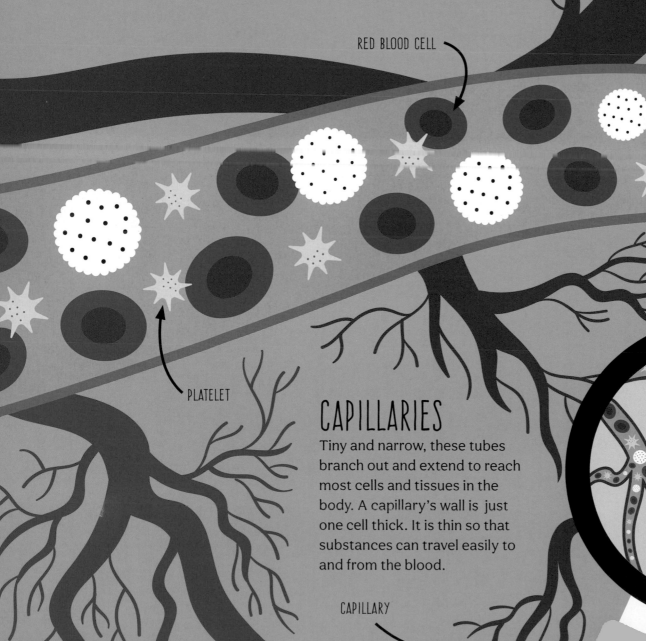

RED BLOOD CELL

PLATELET

## CAPILLARIES

Tiny and narrow, these tubes branch out and extend to reach most cells and tissues in the body. A capillary's wall is just one cell thick. It is thin so that substances can travel easily to and from the blood.

CAPILLARIES

CAPILLARY

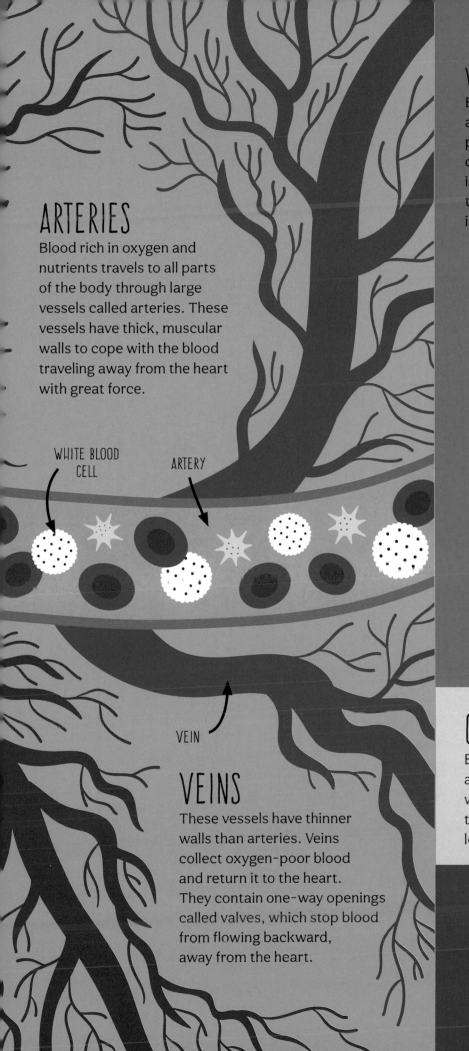

# ARTERIES

Blood rich in oxygen and nutrients travels to all parts of the body through large vessels called arteries. These vessels have thick, muscular walls to cope with the blood traveling away from the heart with great force.

WHITE BLOOD CELL

ARTERY

VEIN

# VEINS

These vessels have thinner walls than arteries. Veins collect oxygen-poor blood and return it to the heart. They contain one-way openings called valves, which stop blood from flowing backward, away from the heart.

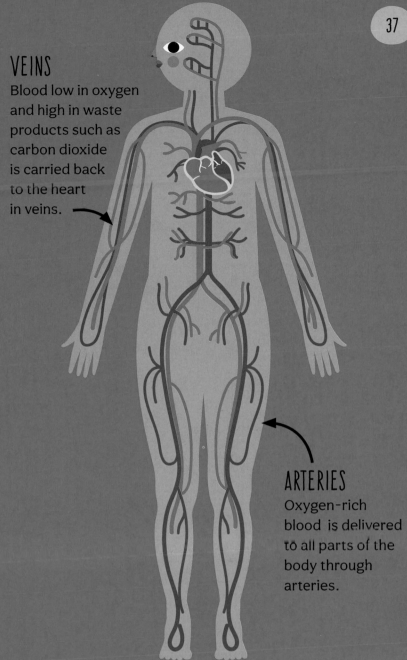

## VEINS
Blood low in oxygen and high in waste products such as carbon dioxide is carried back to the heart in veins.

## ARTERIES
Oxygen-rich blood is delivered to all parts of the body through arteries.

# CIRCULATORY SYSTEM
Blood takes less than a minute to travel around the body and back to the heart, ready to be pumped again. On the way, substances leave and enter the bloodstream, passing through capillaries' very thin walls to and from cells. Blood low in oxygen returns along veins to the heart.

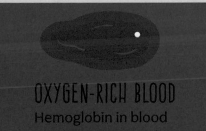

## OXYGEN-RICH BLOOD
Hemoglobin in blood carries oxygen and makes it bright red.

## OXYGEN-POOR BLOOD
Blood low in oxygen is a dark, red-purple color. It is often shown as blue.

# LUNGS

It is essential that the human body has a nonstop supply of oxygen, which is why it needs a pair of lungs.

An average human takes 12–20 breaths or more every minute, even when they are asleep. Each breath carries air into the lungs. This pair of large, spongy sacs is packed full of 30,000 thin tubes called bronchioles, which transport air into every part of these vital organs. The body uses oxygen to help turn food into energy.

AIR IN

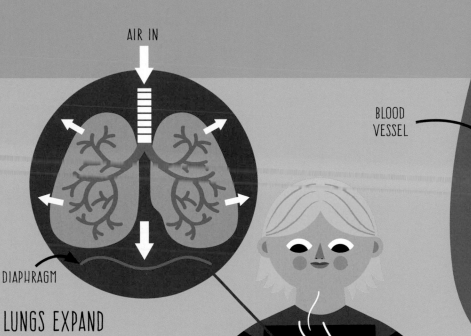

DIAPHRAGM

## LUNGS EXPAND

The diaphragm muscle tightens and moves downward as the rib cage gets larger for the lungs to expand.

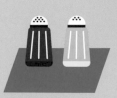

WINDPIPE

RIGHT LUNG

BLOOD VESSEL

BRONCHIOLE

## BREATHING IN

To breathe in, the lungs expand, drawing in air through the nose and mouth. The air travels through the throat and down a tube called the windpipe. It branches in two and these tubes—the left and right bronchus—transport air into the lungs.

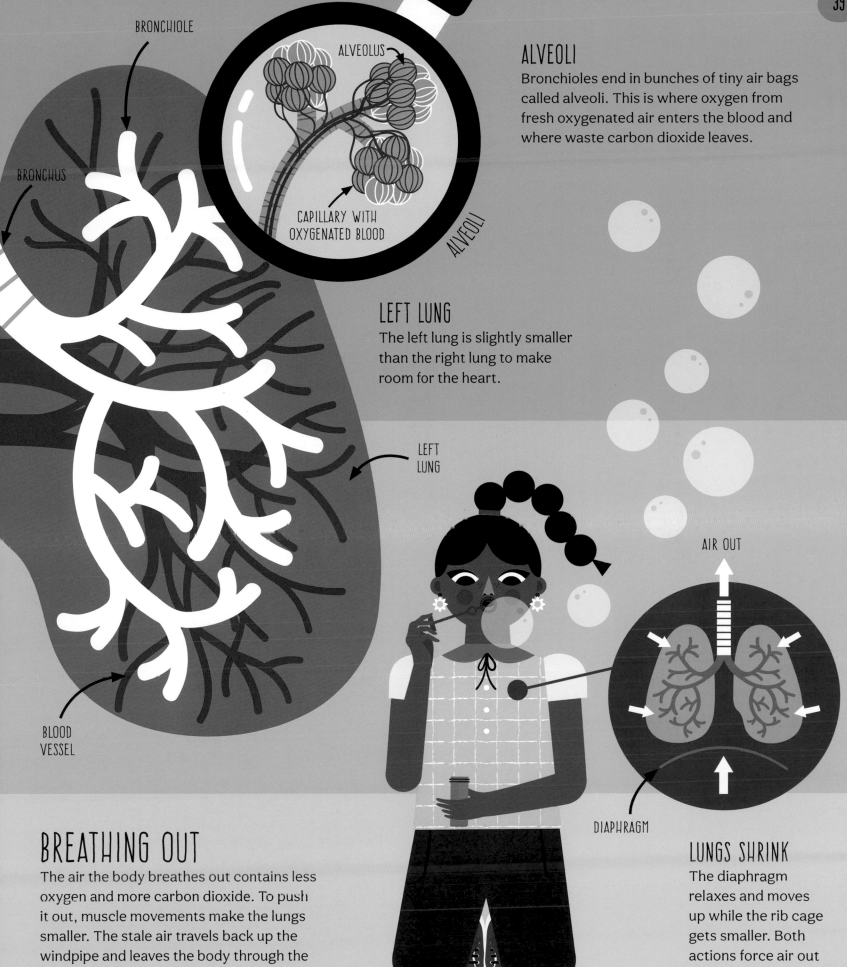

BRONCHIOLE

ALVEOLUS

## ALVEOLI

Bronchioles end in bunches of tiny air bags called alveoli. This is where oxygen from fresh oxygenated air enters the blood and where waste carbon dioxide leaves.

BRONCHUS

CAPILLARY WITH OXYGENATED BLOOD

ALVEOLI

## LEFT LUNG

The left lung is slightly smaller than the right lung to make room for the heart.

LEFT LUNG

AIR OUT

BLOOD VESSEL

DIAPHRAGM

## BREATHING OUT

The air the body breathes out contains less oxygen and more carbon dioxide. To push it out, muscle movements make the lungs smaller. The stale air travels back up the windpipe and leaves the body through the mouth and nose.

## LUNGS SHRINK

The diaphragm relaxes and moves up while the rib cage gets smaller. Both actions force air out of the lungs.

# MOUTH AND TEETH

The mouth is where food goes into the body, so it's the place for the teeth. A human develops two sets of teeth in their lifetime. The first set of 20 baby, or milk, teeth start falling out at age six or so. They are replaced by 32 adult teeth, split equally between the upper and lower jaw. Gums surround the base of each tooth, forming a seal and helping to keep the tooth in place.

But the mouth isn't just important for biting and chewing food. It also allows the body to make a wide range of loud and quiet sounds, and communicate with others in different ways.

## SMILING

A grin widens the mouth and shows the front teeth. A human can move their mouth in many ways to show how they're feeling without talking.

 **MOLARS**
For chewing and grinding.

**M**

 **PREMOLARS**
For tearing, crushing, and grinding.

**P**

 **CANINES**
For ripping and tearing.

**C**

 **INCISORS**
For cutting and slicing.

**I**

• TOP TEETH •

M M M P P C I I I I I C P P M M M

## TOOTH ORDER

Teeth are arranged so that the biting teeth–the incisors– are found at the front. To the rear are the blocky teeth used for crushing and grinding–the premolars and molars.

M M M P P C I I I I I C P P M M M

• BOTTOM TEETH •

## TALKING
Changing the shape of the mouth, lips, and tongue alters the flow of air out of the mouth. This enables different sounds to form speech.

## SINGING
Notes start in the throat when air rushes over two flaps called vocal cords. These vibrate back and forth, creating sounds.

## WHISTLING
The tongue forms a curved shape while muscles in the face purse the lips together. When the mouth blows, the escaping air forms a tuneful whistle.

## HOW MANY TEETH DO HUMANS HAVE?
A typical adult human has 32 permanent teeth.

$$4 + 8 + 8 + 12 = 32$$

canines | premolars | incisors | molars | permanent teeth

## INSIDE A TOOTH
Each tooth is anchored deep into the jawbone by its root. Inside, the pulp cavity is soft, contains nerves and blood vessels, and is surrounded by a bonelike material called dentine. The outer tooth is made of enamel—the hardest substance in the whole body.

**OPEN WIDE!**

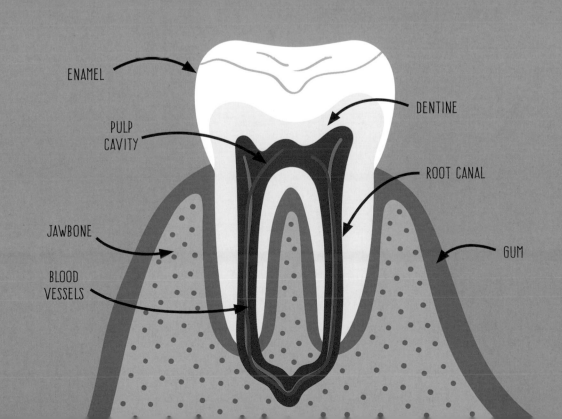

ENAMEL

DENTINE

PULP CAVITY

ROOT CANAL

JAWBONE

GUM

BLOOD VESSELS

# DIGESTIVE SYSTEM

Food in the mouth has to go somewhere—and that somewhere is a series of muscular tubes and pouches. These all need to be connected together to form the digestive system.

This extremely important system takes food on quite a journey, starting from the lower part of the head and ending with the bottom of the body's torso. Along the way, the food is mashed up, churned around, and broken down so its nutrients can be used by the body as fuel, to grow, and for repair. The first part of the process is all about getting the food from the mouth to the stomach.

YUM...

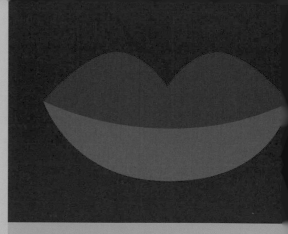

## MOUTH FOR CHEWING

The mouth contains teeth and receives up to a quart of saliva a day to make food wet from six glands on either side of the mouth.

## BOLUS

The mouth forms a ball-shaped lump of food called a bolus. It is wet with saliva and an ideal shape for traveling down tubes.

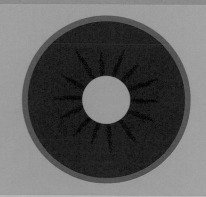

## EATING, CHEWING AND SWALLOWING

The jaw must be equipped with strong muscles to move the mouth and allow its teeth to chew, crush, and grind up food. The tongue, on the mouth's floor, pushes food to the back, ready for swallowing. This action uses more than 20 muscles in the mouth, throat, and esophagus.

## SPHINCTER

Rings of muscle open to let food in and out of the esophagus. The top ring closes tight to stop air entering the esophagus when breathing.

# GULP, GULP

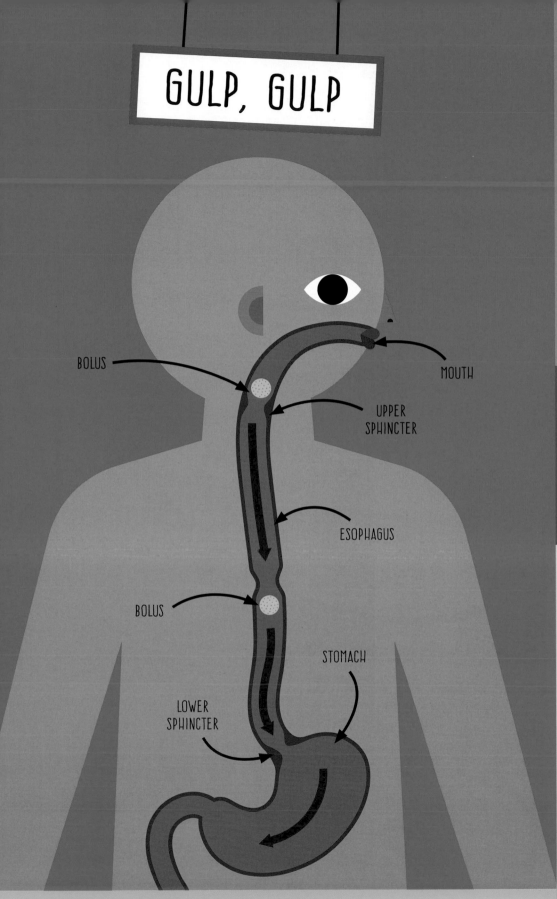

BOLUS

MOUTH

UPPER
SPHINCTER

ESOPHAGUS

BOLUS

STOMACH

LOWER
SPHINCTER

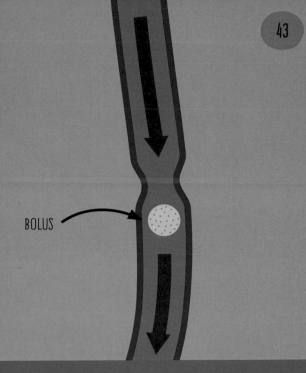

BOLUS

## ESOPHAGUS
Located just behind the body's
windpipe, this tube's muscular
walls squeeze in and out to push
food downward.

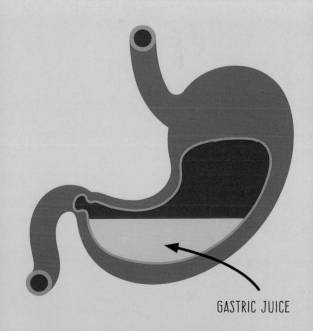

GASTRIC JUICE

## FOOD'S JOURNEY TO THE STOMACH
The mouth and stomach are connected by a 12-inch-long muscular
tube running vertically inside the rib cage. It is called the esophagus. Its
upper sphincter relaxes to admit a bolus of food, and its lower sphincter
relaxes to let the bolus leave the esophagus and enter the stomach.

## STOMACH
Connected to the bottom end of the
esophagus, this stretchy bag is filled
with gastric juice. This acidic liquid
breaks food down into a soupy gloop.

# INTESTINES

The small intestine is the longest single tube in the body and has to be coiled up snugly to fit inside. It is surrounded by the large intestine. The stomach releases its soupy, gloopy liquid into the small intestine. Food moves slowly through its twisting, turning walls, where it is broken down further into small, simple molecules. Then the magic happens. Most of the useful substances in food–from calcium, which keeps bones strong, to sugars, which provide energy–are absorbed into the body. The leftovers travel into the large intestine for more processing.

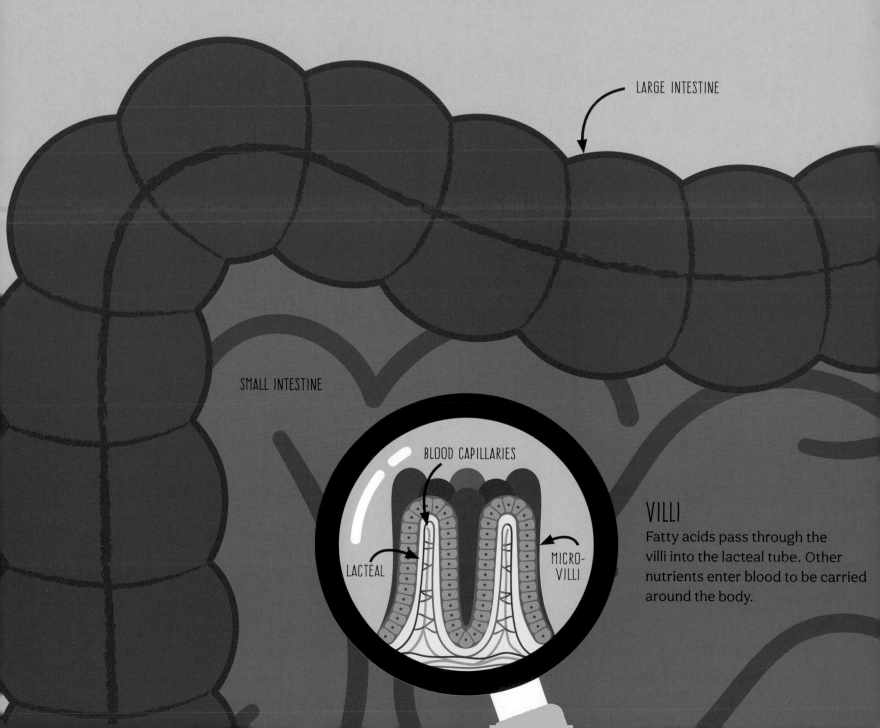

LARGE INTESTINE

SMALL INTESTINE

BLOOD CAPILLARIES

LACTEAL

MICRO-VILLI

## VILLI
Fatty acids pass through the villi into the lacteal tube. Other nutrients enter blood to be carried around the body.

BACTERIA

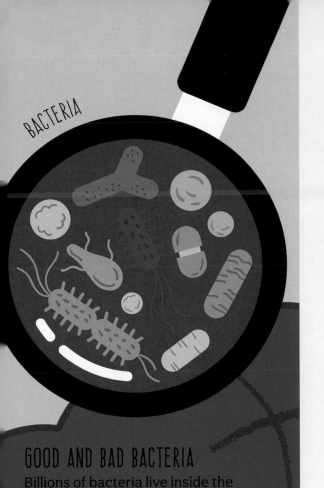

LIVER

GALL
BLADDER

LARGE
INTESTINE

STOMACH

PANCREAS

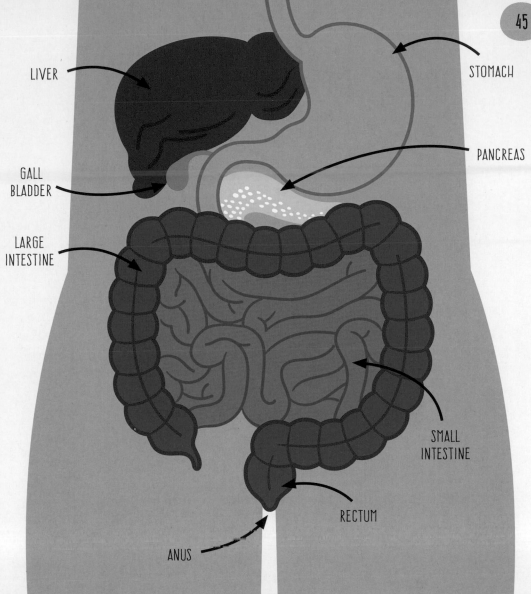

SMALL
INTESTINE

RECTUM

ANUS

## GOOD AND BAD BACTERIA

Billions of bacteria live inside the
intestines. Some cause infections,
but many others help the body digest
food. Some even produce vitamins.

## INSIDE STORY

The small intestine's inner
walls are wrinkly and lined
with millions of tiny fingers
called villi. These increase the
surface area for nutrients to
pass quickly through the villi
and be absorbed by the body.

## BREAKING DOWN FOOD

The small intestine relies on help from two other organs—the pancreas and
the liver. The pancreas injects juice full of chemicals, which break down
the food's sugars and starches. The liver makes bile, which is stored in
the gall bladder. When released into the small intestine, bile works with
pancreatic juice to break down the fats in food.

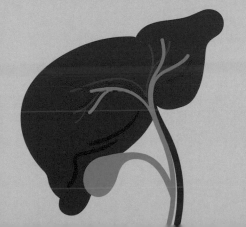

## LIVER

After absorbing nutrients from the small
intestine, blood travels to the liver. This
amazing organ filters out any unwanted
substances and processes the rest into
chemicals the body can use for energy,
growth, and repair.

# REMOVING WASTE

**EAT UP!**

The body has to be able to remove its waste. A hardworking pair of organs called the kidneys are essential for this process.

The remains of a meal may stay in the body for up to 48 hours. For much of this time, it moves slowly through the large intestine. There, water and any remaining nutrients are absorbed into the body, leaving behind solid waste. Other waste, produced from cells, enters the blood and is filtered out by the kidneys.

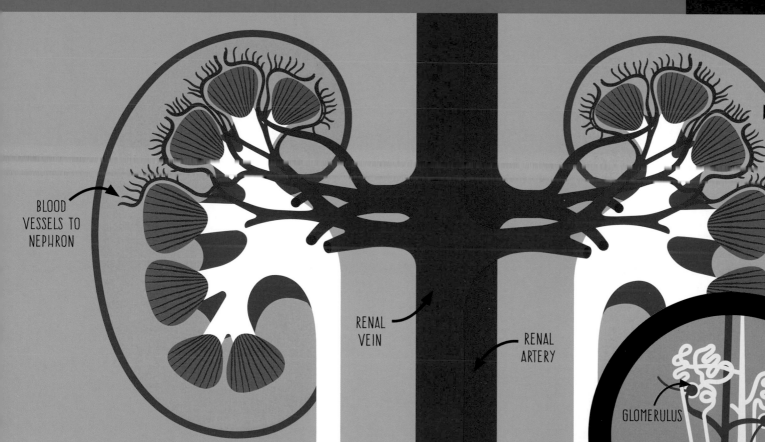

KIDNEY CORTEX

BLOOD VESSELS TO NEPHRON

RENAL VEIN

RENAL ARTERY

NEPHRONS

GLOMERULUS

TUBULE

## THE KIDNEYS

These 4- to 5-inch-long, bean-shaped organs separate out unwanted substances from blood. The cleaned blood travels along the renal vein back to the heart. The liquid waste–called urine–goes to the bladder. Urine contains about 95% water and 5% waste and salt.

## FILTERING UNITS

Around a million little bundles of tubes and blood vessels are found in each kidney. These nephrons filter and clean up to 50 gallons of blood every 24 hours.

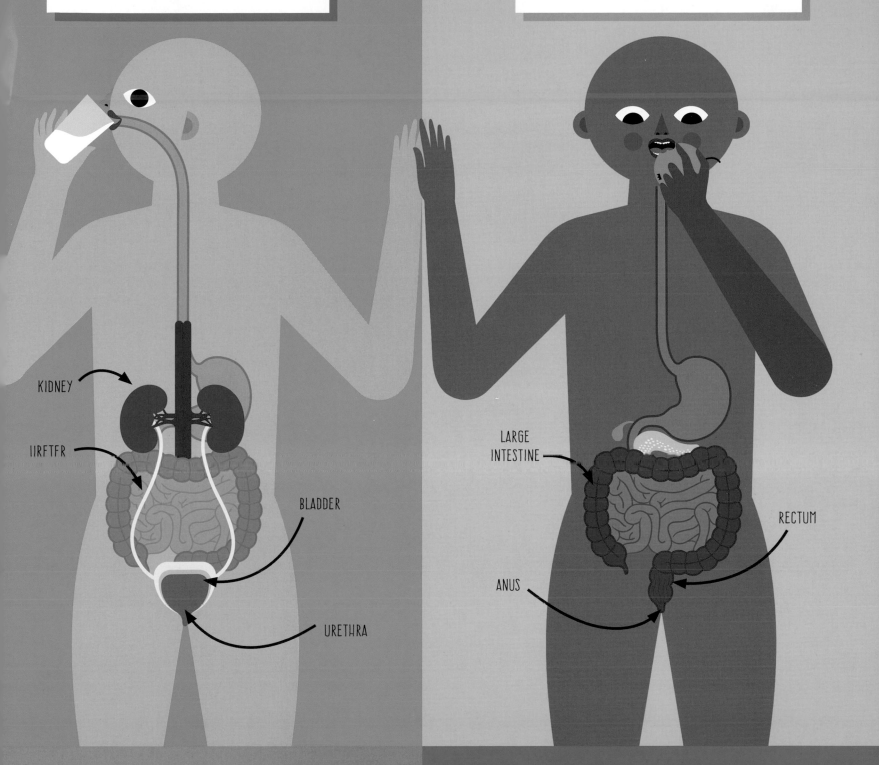

# THE URINARY SYSTEM

As the kidneys do their work, they send more and more urine to the bladder, which expands to hold the liquid. When nearly full, the bladder sends nerve signals telling the brain it's time for a trip to the toilet. The urine exits through the urethra.

# THE WASTE SYSTEM

After liquid and nutrients have been absorbed, the remaining waste is pushed out of the large intestine into the short but wide rectum for storage. When someone visits the toilet, muscles loosen to let the waste leave the body through the anus.

# BODY DEFENDERS

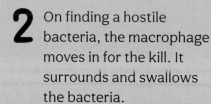

To protect itself from outside threats such as dirt, viruses, and bacteria, the human body needs a built-in defense system.

On the outside, skin and snotty mucus can stop dangerous invaders from traveling too far into the body. But when bacteria, viruses, and other nasties make it inside, special kinds of white blood cells are needed to hunt them down. Many white blood cells are found in blood vessels. But others flow through a network of tubes called the lymphatic system.

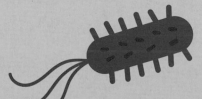

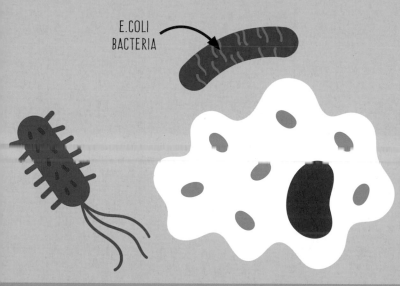

E.COLI BACTERIA

INFLUENZA VIRUS

**1** White blood cells called macrophages act as security guards. They patrol blood and lymph on the lookout for invading germs.

**2** On finding a hostile bacteria, the macrophage moves in for the kill. It surrounds and swallows the bacteria.

## BARRIERS

A number of liquids and reactions can help the human body to stop bacteria and other threats before they get too far. Sweat, for example, contains chemicals that kill some skin bacteria.

### TEARS

Glands above the eyes produce tears. So, every time the eyes blink, a film of salty tears washes away dirt and grit that could scratch the cornea.

### SALIVA

Saliva is important for moistening food. But it also kills some harmful bacteria in the mouth. This helps to fight tooth and gum decay.

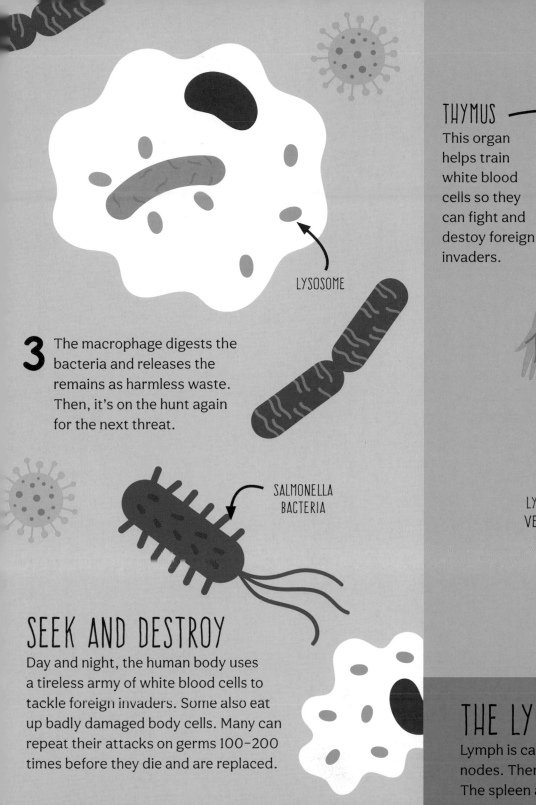

LYSOSOME

**3** The macrophage digests the bacteria and releases the remains as harmless waste. Then, it's on the hunt again for the next threat.

SALMONELLA BACTERIA

# SEEK AND DESTROY

Day and night, the human body uses a tireless army of white blood cells to tackle foreign invaders. Some also eat up badly damaged body cells. Many can repeat their attacks on germs 100–200 times before they die and are replaced.

THYMUS
This organ helps train white blood cells so they can fight and destoy foreign invaders.

LYMPH NODE

SPLEEN

LYMPH VESSEL

# LYMPH
A watery fluid called lymph flows through the lymphatic system. It is full of white blood cells, which attack harmful bacteria in body tissues and blood.

# THE LYMPHATIC SYSTEM

Lymph is carried through tubes to filters called lymph nodes. There, white blood cells destroy germs in the lymph. The spleen acts as the largest lymph node in the body.

# MUCUS

This sticky fluid lines the mouth, throat, nose, and other body parts. It traps germs, dust, and grit, stopping them spreading through the body.

# HAY FEVER

Some bodies' defenses overreact to harmless threats, such as pollen from plants. The defenses cause the eyes and nose to swell up and run.

SWEAT PORE

# SKIN, HAIR, AND NAILS

Skin is the body's outer covering and its largest organ by far. It is waterproof, keeps out germs, and protects against the Sun's harmful rays. Brilliant! It also helps control the body's temperature and lets a person sense their surroundings by touch and feel. Millions of fine hairs cover the skin and help keep it warm by trapping a layer of air. The skin is constantly repaired and renewed as dead skin cells on the outer surface are shed and new cells take their place.

## SWEAT GLAND
This releases watery sweat out of tiny holes in the skin called pores. Sweating helps the body cool down.

SWEAT GLAND

BLOOD VESSEL

FAT TISSUE

## HEAD HAIR
If a human has healthy hair follicles, around 100,000 hairs will grow on the head. They are thicker than body hairs.

## EYELASHES
These fine eyelid hairs trap dirt and dust. If touched, they trigger the eyelid to close to protect the eye.

## EYEBROWS
A pair of hairy mats help soak up sweat running down the forehead to stop it reaching the eye.

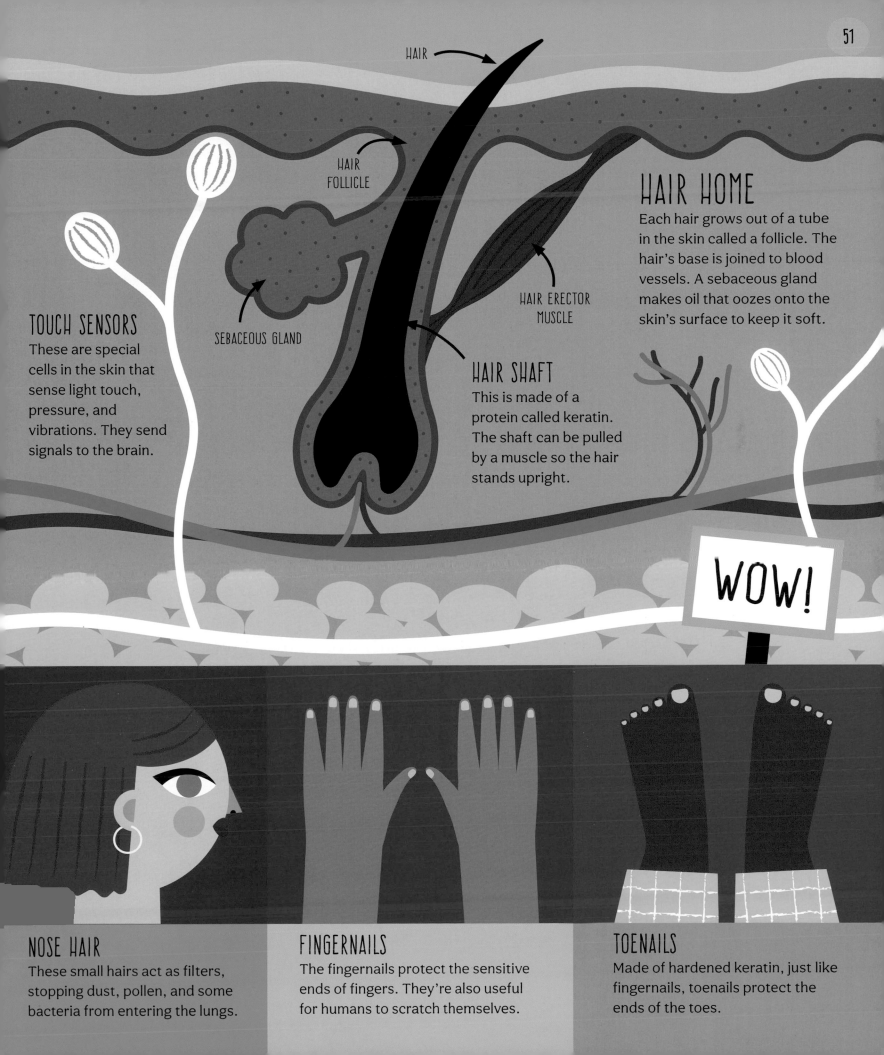

HAIR

HAIR FOLLICLE

HAIR ERECTOR MUSCLE

SEBACEOUS GLAND

## TOUCH SENSORS

These are special cells in the skin that sense light touch, pressure, and vibrations. They send signals to the brain.

## HAIR SHAFT

This is made of a protein called keratin. The shaft can be pulled by a muscle so the hair stands upright.

## HAIR HOME

Each hair grows out of a tube in the skin called a follicle. The hair's base is joined to blood vessels. A sebaceous gland makes oil that oozes onto the skin's surface to keep it soft.

WOW!

## NOSE HAIR

These small hairs act as filters, stopping dust, pollen, and some bacteria from entering the lungs.

## FINGERNAILS

The fingernails protect the sensitive ends of fingers. They're also useful for humans to scratch themselves.

## TOENAILS

Made of hardened keratin, just like fingernails, toenails protect the ends of the toes.

# HAIR AND SKIN

From the outside, each body tends to look a little bit different—from differing heights and facial features to varying skin and hair colors. These differences make every human special and unique and easier to recognize.

Color is created by special cells in the skin and hair follicles called melanocytes. They produce a group of chemicals called melanin, which are color-creating substances, also known as pigment. The melanin passes into neighboring cells, coloring them. The more melanin produced, the darker the color. As skin cells flake off and hairs fall out, melanocytes have to continue producing melanin. In some bodies, melanin production reduces as the body ages, causing white or gray hair.

## BEAUTY SPOTS

Moles are sometimes called beauty spots! They are bundles of melanocyte cells and can be black, brown, or pink.

## FRECKLES

These little marks are small clumps of pigment cells. They show up faces and arms.

## STRAIGHT HAIR

Follicles can be circular or oval. Circular follicles that point straight up are likely to grow straight hair.

## WAVY HAIR

Somewhere between straight and curly, this type of hair can form loose "S"-shaped patterns if grown long.

## CURLY HAIR

Follicles that are oval or grow at an angle to the skin's surface are more likely to produce curly hair.

## MUSTACHE

An option for some bodies is to grow a strip of facial hair, or mustache, above the top lip.

## BLUSHING

When a human is embarrassed, blood rushes faster through blood vessels under the skin, causing a red face.

## BEARD

For a human to have a beard on its face, chin, or throat, it needs plenty of facial hair follicles.

## SKIN TONE

Melanocytes create a body's skin color. Exposure to strong sunlight can stimulate the skin's melanocytes to produce extra melanin. This may darken the skin color further to protect it from harmful ultraviolet, or UV, rays found in sunlight.

## COILED HAIR

For small, tight "S"-shaped curls that are dense and springy, hair follicles need to be oval and sharply angled.

## RED HAIR

Extra amounts of reddish melanin pigment produced by hair follicles can give a red or ginger hair color.

# HOW TO LOOK AFTER A HUMAN

A human body doesn't just need all its bits and pieces in the right places. It needs looking after, too. It needs fuel to power all its systems, to grow, and to move around. It needs regular exercise to keep its bones and muscles strong. Washing and bathing help keep harmful germs and infections away. Rest and sleep give the body's systems a chance to slow down, repair themselves, and recover after a day's work.

If it's looked after well, a human can develop new skills and abilities, connect with other humans, learn about the world, and do lots of other marvelous and exciting things.

# EAT AND DRINK

## FRUIT AND VEGETABLES

These important foods contain lots of vitamins and minerals. They're also full of fiber, which helps digestion.

VEGETABLES

FRUIT

## PROTEIN

Used by the body for growth and repair, protein helps build muscles, too.

FISH

MEAT

EGG

NUTS

The body needs plenty of fuel to digest and turn into energy. A balanced diet has a good mixture of different food types, which together give the body all the nutrients it needs to stay healthy. A good diet avoids too much salt, sugar, or fat.

## WATER

To work at its best, the body needs 2–3 quarts of water a day. It gets about a quarter of this from food.

YAMS

## CARBOHYDRATES

These sugars and starches are converted into glucose. They are then carried in blood to provide fuel to all the body's cells.

BREAD

OIL

CHEESE

## FATS

Found in dairy products, oil, meat, and some fish, fats act as a store of energy for the body.

BUTTER

RICE

PASTA

# EXERCISE

## SPORTS
Playing games is very good exercise. It makes the heart and lungs push blood faster around the body.

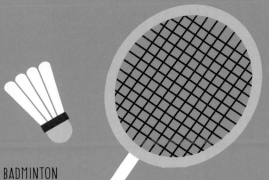

BADMINTON

BALLET

TENNIS

TAP SHOES

## DANCE
Ballet, tap, and other dance can improve fitness and body flexibility. Stretching can give the body even more range of movement.

All those mighty muscles, including the heart, need a good, regular workout. Exercise helps keep muscles strong. It also gives the body stamina—the ability to work hard for long periods of time. Keeping fit helps keep bones strong and joints moving and flexible, too.

FOOTBALL

SOCCER

## CYCLING
This is a fun way to keep fit. It helps exercise the heart, lungs, and leg muscles, especially when riding up hills.

HIKING BOOTS

WATER BOTTLE

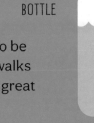

BICYCLE

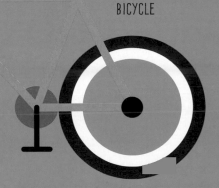

## WALKING
Exercise doesn't have to be fast and furious. Long walks at a good speed can be great for the body, too.

# WASH

## CLEAN, DRY CLOTHES

Wearing damp, dirty, or sweaty clothes for days in a row can allow fungus and other germs to grow and cause infections. Humans need to change and wash clothes regularly.

A clean body is a healthy body. Washing stops build-ups of bacteria and other harmful germs that can cause infections and health problems. Cleaning includes washing hands regularly, especially after coughing, sneezing, or going to the toilet.

SOAP

## CLEANING TEETH AND GUMS

Brushing teeth removes bacteria and the old food they feast on. Left to thrive, bacteria will make acid, which leads to decay.

## WASHING EVERY DAY

Soap and warm water remove dried sweat, dirt, and bacteria from all parts of the body. They make it smell better, too!

## FIRST AID

Everyday cuts, grazes, and scrapes to the body can be cleaned and treated at home. Over time, new skin will grow over wounds.

FIRST AID BOX

BANDAGES

CREAM

THERMOMETER

The human body is pretty amazing at repairing itself. For example, it replaces worn-out skin cells regularly and changes all the cells that line the intestines every 5–7 days. But sometimes, the body needs medical help to heal.

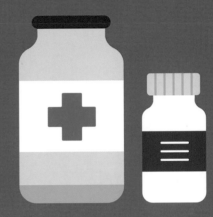

MEDICINE

## MEDICAL EXPERTS

Sometimes, doctors and other experts are needed to examine bodies that aren't working. They can give treatments and medicines.

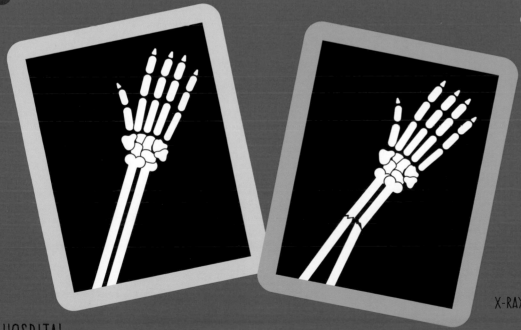

X-RAYS

## HOSPITAL

X-ray machines and other devices look inside bodies to see what's wrong. Problems can often be removed or corrected with an operation.

STETHOSCOPE

# SLEEP

## BEDTIME ROUTINE
The body is tired by the evening and needs to rest at night. It is important that it gets enough sleep.

The human body can't run at full speed all day and all night. It needs rest so that its many systems can slow down, repair themselves, and recover. A good night's sleep leaves the body refreshed and ready for action the next day.

## DREAMS
All humans have dreams. But scientists aren't sure what they are for. Maybe dreams occur as the brain makes memories, refreshes itself, and tries to understand what's happened that day.

## SLEEPING
The body's breathing and heart rate drop when it is asleep, so the heart and lungs work less hard. A human needs to to sleep for 7-12 hours a night.

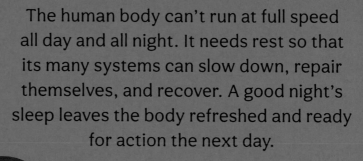

GROW AND DEVELOP

## TEENAGER
More changes occur as the body develops from a child into an adult.

Looked after and fed well, the body grows and develops quickly. Of course, a human can't actually be built by another human. A baby is born and grows into a child, who develops into a teenager. The teenager then becomes an adult who changes in all sorts of ways as it gets older.

## CHILD
The body learns new skills, makes new friends, thinks up ideas, and grows taller and stronger.

## ADULT
The body is fully developed but will continue to change as it grows older over a lifetime that may last 80 years or more.

## BABY
A baby can laugh, cry, and recognize faces. It starts learning how to control its body movements.

## TODDLER
It's a busy time for the body as it learns to speak its first words, crawl, walk, and sense the world.

# GLOSSARY

### ARTERY
A tube that carries blood rich in oxygen away from the heart to other parts of the body.

### BACTERIA
Tiny living things made of a single cell. Some are useful to the human body, but others can be harmful.

### BLADDER
A stretchy, muscular pouch that stores urine in between toilet visits.

### CAPILLARY
A tiny blood vessel that is smaller than an artery.

### CARBON DIOXIDE
An invisible gas that is made by cells as a waste product. It leaves the body when a person breathes out.

### CELL
One of the tiny living building blocks that make up parts of a human body.

### COMMUNICATE
To pass on or share information with others.

### DIAPHRAGM
A large muscle below the lungs that moves up and down to help the body to breathe.

### DIGESTIVE SYSTEM
A system of organs that takes in food and processes it for the body to make energy.

### FOLLICLE
The tiny hole in the skin that surrounds a hair.

### GLAND
An organ that produces a chemical that is used in some way in the body.

### HORMONES
Chemicals that act as messengers as they are sent around the body.

### INFECTION
A disease caused by germs invading the body.

### IRIS
The colored ring around the pupil, or center, of the eye. Muscles in the iris can make the pupil bigger or smaller.

### JOINT
A point where two bones meet. Many joints in the body are moveable.

### KIDNEYS
A pair of organs that filter and clean blood and make urine.

### MELANIN
A pigment that gives the body its skin, hair, and eye color.

## MOLECULE
A group of two or more tiny particles called atoms joined together by chemical bonds.

## NERVES
A bundle of long fibers made up of nerve cells. Many nerves carry signals to and from the brain.

## NUTRIENTS
Substances needed by the body to stay healthy, grow, repair, and work well. Examples include proteins, fats, carbohydrates, vitamins, and minerals.

## OESOPHAGUS
A long tube that carries food from the throat to the stomach.

## ORGAN
A body part made of a group of different tissues that work together to do the same job. Eyes, kidneys, lungs, and the brain are all organs.

## OXYGEN
A colorless gas found in the air. It is used by the body to make energy from food.

## PUPIL
The black circle in the center of the eye that lets light in.

## RETINA
A thin layer of cells at the back of the eye that detect light.

## SKELETON
The frame inside the human body, made up of more than 200 bones.

## SPINAL CORD
A long column of nerve fibers that run from the head down the back. They connect nerves in the body with the brain.

## TENDON
A strap or cord of tissue that connects muscles to bones.

## TISSUE
A group of similar cells that work together. For example, groups of muscle cells form muscle fiber tissue. Groups of nerve cells, or neurons, form nervous tissue.

## VEIN
A blood vessel that carries blood low in oxygen back to the heart.

## VIRUS
Tiny germs that can invade cells. Some can cause illnesses such as flu and chickenpox.

## VITAMINS
A group of substances that are vital for the body's growth and repair and allow it to work well.

## WHITE BLOOD CELL
A type of cell found in blood that fights infection.

# INDEX